Don't Hold Back

EMMA-JANE TAYLOR

VISION MAKER PRESS

Don't Hold Back

Copyright © Emma-Jane Taylor 2018

ISBN 978-1-9995849-4-8

First Published October 2018

Imprint - Emma-Jane Taylor

Designed, Printed & Published by Vision Maker Press

Printed in Great Britain by www.visionmakerpress.com

Front cover photograph credit Zelda de Hollander, Studio Shotz

Dedication

For the women and men in the world fighting for emotional freedom, you can do it! You are worth it! Have faith, trust in yourself and ride your wave with conviction.

Don't Hold Back

Contents

Testimonials for *Don't Hold Back*

Emma-Jane and I had our daughters two weeks apart and we have all been best friends ever since. As you can tell from this book, Emma-Jane's key focus is to bring her daughter up to be a strong, confident woman surrounded by love and happiness. I think that most people, including myself, have had experience of childhood abuse in some form, and unfortunately the most vulnerable children who are already experiencing so much heartache are those targets. I am so proud of Emma-Jane for giving a voice to this subject and the effects it has on you for your whole life and offering the tools to deal with it. She has achieved so much in her adult life and is continuing to grow and move on with her life goals. She is truly inspirational.

Aimee Laming

I love the way Emma-Jane speaks with such an open heart and bears all of this in this raw and authentic manner. It shows true courage. This in turn helps you to look inside and look at the darker things in life you may run and hide from. Once you have opened that up she gives you some great tools to help you on your journey to heal. This book is full of thought-provoking questions that will have you delving deep into your own mind.

Lisa Walker - Life's Little Puzzles

As an adult survivor of childhood sexual abuse, I cannot recommend Emma-Jane's Taylor's, *Don't Hold Back* enough.
Her story is horrifying and gripping, loving and gentle, empowering and inspiring. It shows us how we can live peaceful lives full of abundance and the love we crave. I recommend this book to anyone who just needs a little help here and of course... there is no shame in doing so.

Lucy Swift

Don't Hold Back

In this book, Emma-Jane speaks from her heart and her own experiences. This allows her to take you by the hand and guide you from dark to light on your journey to recovery. I am lucky enough to know Emma-Jane and have witnessed her positive and nurturing nature; she is determined to help and heal you. She holds you in her gentle embrace and gives you a tool box to make your dreams a reality. Thank you, Emma-Jane for supporting me on my path to a bright future.

Juliet Cox

I felt like *Don't Hold Back* was speaking to my soul at a time I needed it most. The words spoke to me on a deep level and they were exactly what I needed to hear during a difficult time in my life. It is the perfect read when you need to find some strength: I marked certain pages so I could revisit the gems of positivity again!

This is a book not just to read but to act on. It is full of practical tips and exercises to help you on your journey. I have learnt so many valuable lessons.

Imogen Scott

Don't Hold Back

Acknowledgments

I would like to thank many people in my life. Firstly, my parents Jane and Alan Taylor for always loving me and believing in me throughout the good and bad times; they are more than my parents, they are my rocks, my friends and have always believed in me.

My amazing friends (*they know who they are*) for always being there. Thank you for believing in me and giving me the best support a girl can ask for.

To all the professionals who have, and who continue, to support me: I sincerely thank you all for helping me find my strengths, positivity and love in my heart and soul.

Last but by no means least, thank you to my beautiful daughter. She is my best-friend, my energy and my reason for living - she completes me. Everything I do is driven by my desire to give my daughter and others a strength that may be missing from life; offering better opportunities and awareness.

If I am proof that you can survive in life, then I hope I can also become my daughter's inspiration too. I am truly blessed by some of the greatest support, thank you to you all!

Stepping forward to share my personal story on being sexually abused and abandoned as a child is something I have thought long and hard about for many years. I didn't take this decision to go public, lightly. I wrote and deleted many times before I got here to this point of sharing my published book with you.

My life is now a beautiful existence in a world that has educated me to appreciate what I have and to believe in better days. Every moment has been a learning curve, even the toughest of times have given me hope. Never doubt your journey; there is a reason for everything. Remember, there really is nothing simple as you start this journey; don't plan anything, just go with the 'flow'. Keep positive and see where it leads you!

So, all there is to say is thank you for taking the time to read my book, please do get in touch with me, I would really like to hear from you, and please don't hide. It is your time.

Don't Hold Back.

Acknowledgments

Don't Hold Back

Foreword

I've known Emma-Jane for a while now but, like anyone who knows her, I knew *of* her long before we met. Focused. Driven. Force of nature. These are words you will often hear.

And there's a misconception that people with such entrepreneurial spirit are simply made that way, that they are a certain type of person or they are born into a privilege that affords them the opportunity to take risks where others would not. These can be true, of course, but reading *Don't Hold Back* offers a different route to personal, emotional, financial and physical success and freedom that will help you to understand another word you will regularly hear about its author: inspirational.

It may not be the story you are expecting. There is struggle and abuse and abandonment. There are troubles and wrong decisions and heartache.

I've been working with people for years to help change their lifestyles to something that is healthier, happier and can be paid forward to those around them - which is the only avenue to true fulfilment. The overriding similarity between these people is that they are stuck; something has occurred that they can't seem to let go of and it drags them down. This can range from the death of a family member to discontent with a career choice. It can be anything from being bullied at school to family differences to the breakdown of a loving relationship. They are issues that all of us will face at some time or another and to varying degrees of severity.

In order to change your story, you must change your state, your approach. This change does not have to be gradual, it can be instant. But most of the time it is difficult to see where that change should be or how you can achieve it. One way to success, to making positive and lasting change, is to find somebody who has already done it. Watch them. Learn from them. Make them your mentor. And then do it quicker.

This book is not a mantra or a positive statement or a motivational poster. It's an honest and heartfelt account of hardship from an early age, how it can create negativity and how that manifests itself through time into further distress. But, more importantly, it is about taking back control. It's about using failures as lessons. It is about ditching the guilt and rubbish and extraneous from your life in order to reclaim it. It's about filling your time with the things and the people that bring out the best.

This is a handbook for anyone ready to let go and take that first step forwards. To not hold themselves back or be held back by another. To realise that the person you were does not have to be the person you are.

So, read this. Learn from it. Stop the suffering. Find something to appreciate. Give *yourself* the opportunity to be inspiring, to be more driven, to become your own force of nature. Do it. Do it now. Don't hold back.

Wayne Pittaway
Author (Will Carver)
Novels – Girl 4, The Two, The Killer Inside, Dead Set

Preface

Dear Reader,

Being ourselves, following our dreams and identifying the right and wrong people in our lives will bring a feeling of contentment that so many of us need. I know first-hand that holding onto a life that is making you feel unhappy is not productive.

When I was 9 years old I found myself snowballing out of control with a series of emotional and physical events that left me unable to function as a teenager and young adult. After a watershed moment in my early 20's I decided to take stock.

At 22 years old I started my own business and I also started my therapy, or as I now like to call it, *my recovery*. It seemed a lot to cope with but each one (business and recovery) seemed to compliment the other and helped me push through some difficult times. I soon discovered that I needed to let go of the person within me – the person I had held on to so tightly, for so long, but who wasn't making me happy, yet the person I felt that I should be. I started to understand that life could be much happier and fulfilled and, although a tough ride, it was becoming a worthwhile journey. And my journey has given me strength, peace, happiness, understanding, purpose, determination, an enriched life and an engaged spirit.

I am now a 40-something-year-old woman who has finally caught up with herself. I am a Mother first, and then a business woman.

I finally feel at peace with who I am and where I am going in my life; it is an exciting time and one I am finally ready for.

Emma-Jane Taylor
The Inspirational Mentor

Introduction

*Life might not always be perfect, but it is beautiful, and we must
find that beauty to see clearly
– Emma-Jane Taylor –*

How many times in your life have you wished that you hadn't
held back? Wished that you could have stood up and done all the
things that you had wanted to do without feeling like you were
letting others down or feeling out of place and worrying about
what others thought of you? Are you simply not true to yourself
for fear of failure or guilt? Or have you struggled to identify with
who you are and just lost sight of your life?

My book reflects my story of rejection, abandonment, low self-
esteem, lack of confidence and how my vulnerability gave me my
strength, my career and the life I have created for myself, now.

So many of us pull our *invisible blankets* over our heads and think,
'this will be ok'. We believe that it will shut away our problems and
that life will be good. But sadly, it rarely is. It simply continues
to allow us to live unhappily in our silent bubble full of fear,
despair and nerves. I know this because I did just that for most
of my growing up years. I thought being silent would give me
power, a strength that I needed to survive, but it didn't. Instead it
weakened my resolve and created insecurity, low self-esteem and
fear. I was a nervous wreck at the best of times and more than flaky
on a functioning day-to-day basis. I lived with night terrors and
struggled to sleep. It was a terrifying time waking up in the night,
full of fear. I used to think my heart would escape me or I would
have a heart attack; it was such a strong physical feeling. I found

myself panicking if I woke in total darkness and, consequently, had to sleep with my light on well into my thirties.

I wrote *Don't Hold Back* to help those who might identify with some of my feelings and emotions and for anyone going through hardships as I did in my earlier years. I hit rock bottom very early on in my life (around 15 or 16 years old) but I really didn't know it at the time. I used to look back over my life and wonder how I could have been that person, the girl who was so desperately sad, lonely, scared, bulimic and suicidal. It doesn't seem possible. But it is. I was that girl. I was terrified of living, scared of people and scared to say the wrong thing for fear of the consequences; I couldn't make decisions, I was emotionally fatigued and a nervous child, shaky and permanently nauseous. Even now, in my forties, I thoroughly think through my options before I make any decisions. I have a voice, I use it and I don't hold back. If I feel it, it is out there. I learnt the hard way and know the consequences of not using my voice.

My first bit of advice to anyone reading this book is to not shy away from who you are, where you have come from or where you want to be in your life. Confronting my fears and taking the necessary time to indulge in myself gave me the strength I so desperately needed to break through. I really want to help you do the same. I hadn't realised until more recently in life how positively my life turned around during my recovery. It took time to adjust and allow changes to my life. But I can honestly look back and see how my years of recovery helped me rediscover the girl I am today - the girl that had been so lost and afraid.

I stepped out of many comfort zones to get to where I am today, and I did it through channelling my sadness and negativity, by turning all my negatives and sadness into mental strength, dedication and a desire to live a better and happier life. I understood early on that I couldn't fight pain with pain. I had to let the pain teach me and help me recover. It was tough. Some days were so painful and so mentally destroying I honestly wasn't sure how I would get through, or where I would end up.

These days, my emotions will cut off once I start to feel the pain or stress from anyone or any situation that emotionally challenges me (whether that be professionally or personally) or a situation that I don't feel I can trust. I step back and take time to allow myself to make my decisions with a clearer head. It is how I now live my life and it is how my life has shaped me. I always talk things through. It might not always be right, but it is clearer and functional for me and that is how I live and work. I am a happy woman with a beautiful daughter in a job I love.

I was very immature and naïve as a child and young adult and I didn't understand what had happened to me, especially how poorly I had been treated. But I now recognise that I was a very troubled child who had reached a very low point and I can see how it had affected my life and how easy it would've been to not be here today writing this book. I feel like I have had a second chance in life, a second wind and I am not going to waste this opportunity for living. I use the lessons I have learnt thus far in life to give me the happiness I so desperately craved as a child, as well as to help others.

I am armed with over 35 years of experience, knowledge, therapy and self-help. This book has been in me since I was 9 years old just waiting for the right time. Although, to be honest, I don't really know if there is ever a right time? What I do know is that one day I just picked up my laptop and wrote (and didn't delete it as I had done so many times previously.)

Since I started this journey, I have also started to speak out in public about my life story. I am gaining momentum and confidence in sharing my story and offering my motivational advice. I am not scared anymore. It is ok. I have been overwhelmed by the response and the many people approaching me since I have stepped forward. I feel proud and quite humble that many people have stepped forward to share their experiences with me and they have felt inspired by me to do so. It really does make my journey and recovery process worthwhile. I've always said that if I can help one person, then it makes me feel proud.

If I was ever scared before about taking my story public, I am not now. It has been liberating to let go and be me, the girl who was trapped within a sea of darkness for many years. Life is really starting to open-up and change direction. There are more opportunities available and all because I am finally allowing me to be me. I am speaking up and out. And whilst a little terrifying, you know what...it is ok!

I have spent many years working on my mental strength, learning about who I really am and how I fit into my life and my surroundings. It hasn't been an easy journey by any stretch of the imagination, but my years thus far have given me the best tools to make the most of my life. I really hope to be able to help you turn your life around, give you food for thought and for you to become the person you have always wished to be, fulfilling your dreams and ambitions with an abundance of self-confidence and happiness.

I absolutely hate to think anyone is suffering in silence, unsure of where or who to turn to, or how to implement changes. So, if I can give any support, tips or advice to anyone feeling like they have lost their way, then it will have all been worth it. I accept my path and make the very best out of everything I now do in life. Every lesson is an education, whether it is a good one or bad. It is all part of our education in life.

I was recently asked in a BBC 3 documentary, what my biggest regret was. I try not to have regrets as I believe life is a lesson. But having to provide a response, the answer was simple: I regret not speaking out sooner!

One thing I wish to share is this; it is important for me to tell you that I certainly don't claim to know everything. Everyone has a story, it is all relative. But what I do know is that you must never give up on yourself, you must keep the faith and the fight within you. I have also learnt how important it is to get professional help; you must talk to people (it might be necessary to speak to your GP). Also, discover how forgiveness is key to recovery, find your tribe and develop your trust and belief in the loved ones around you.

Finding ourselves enhances our lives, brings loved one's closer to our soul and allows us to develop trust, clarity and happiness with a more focused and positive direction. My story might not have been the best start, but it has given me so much and I can now enjoy my life with my loved ones around me.

I truly hope you find, *Don't Hold Back* motivational and I wish you well on your soul-searching journey.

Emma-Jane Taylor x

My Story

When I started this section, I wasn't sure where or how to really start. I have never ever written, my life story down on paper before.

However, I do see this book as part of my 'life' journey and I guess the easiest place for me to start is by saying life took its toll on me as a child and, sadly, my earliest memories were some of my toughest experiences. However, as a wiser more confident adult I can see with greater clarity and reflect more objectively.

When I was around 9-years-old, whilst on a family holiday, I was sexually abused one evening by the Greek restaurant owner. The restaurant was just across the road from our hotel and we had been there as a family on a few occasions before the abuse took place. The male owner and his brother used to entertain the families with Greek dancing, plate throwing, good music and then, when the families or the parents were eating, they would take the children away from their parents to the rear of the restaurant to see their farm animals. These men were (seemingly) nice men; friendly, funny and they appeared to genuinely enjoy looking after the families who ate with them. I remember them smiling and laughing all the time and I distinctively remember liking them both, which I later found very confusing.

On this particular evening, a week or so into our holiday, the owner and his brother took me from my parents (my Mother and Stepfather) as he had done on other occasions whilst they were eating, and we walked off into the warm night with a few other children towards the farm animals. I remember that it was dark. I remember that I felt safe, that it was really warm. One of my little holiday friends was in the group and I can still remember the smell from the farmyard. We were around 20-30 metres from where our parents were dining, so not far. I could clearly see the restaurant and I could still hear the music. I was excited to see the animals; I just adored all animals. I chatted and laughed with the other children and I was smiling as we arrived. I stood next to the man who was crouched beside me, holding my hand tightly and I remember looking back at the restaurant. At that moment I felt safe, I was happy, I was a 9-year-old. I could hear the laughing and I could clearly still see the light from the Taverna...but somehow the light never quite reached the shadows where we were standing...

Next, I remember shaking and running back to the light, to the restaurant and into the bathroom, locking myself in the toilet. I knew I felt dirty, but I just didn't know why... no-one saw me running back to the bathroom and I had no clue about what had just happened. But I was breathless and panicky and knew something was wrong.

This tragic incident was the trigger for my nerves and my obsession with cleanliness. I now bath every night before I go to bed.

I never told anyone of this night until I started my therapy, aged 22.

Feeling wholeheartedly confused and vulnerable (but not saying anything to anyone) I continued to live my life, but I can recollect starting to play up at junior school. My brain seemed to want to block out this incident in Greece and sadly my memory is still limited after this time. I was very scared to speak to anyone, I do remember that, which seems crazy! I started to feel more and more nervous. I became a shaky child, who always needed to go to the bathroom. Our neighbours used to call me, *Emmy-Loo* as I used to go so frequently; little did they know that this was only the start of my many turbulent years.

I didn't really know much about my parents' relationship, other than I used to enjoy seeing my biological Father every other weekend. Some of my earliest and happiest memories were of the weekends I would spend with my Father. My parents had separated when I was 3-years-old, and my Stepfather lived with us and raised me. When I was about 11 or 12-years-old, my life changed once again.

I had just started senior school and it was the weekend to see my Father, I idolised him and was excited to see him. He was my *hero*: he made me laugh, had the best cuddles and a smile that would melt my heart. He had a twinkle in his eye, was cheeky and funny - I just adored this man. However, on this day my Father had an upsetting conversation with me, articulating that his relationship with me was difficult. I wasn't really sure what that meant until the next day, when he told me on the phone that he could no longer have a relationship with me until I was older. I put the phone down and remember running up the road with my Mother and Stepfather in hot pursuit, almost wrestling me and my tears to the floor. And that was that: in the blink of an eye the hero, had gone. I was devastated at losing my Father from my life. And it turned out to be just that.

This is something that has affected my relationships ever since. I knew there were rumblings in the family, but even now I can't understand how any rumblings could lead you to give up your children? Fight harder if you have to, but never give up on your children.

This day in my life haunted me. One minute I had my Father in my life, the next he was gone! For as long as I live, I will never truly understand why?

I haven't had a relationship with my Father or his family since. I felt, for many years, it was my fault that he left, but maturity has helped me understand that he was the adult and I was the child. I struggled to make decisions for a very long time after my Father left for fear of the consequences. Life became a sea of darkness, I was a nervous wreck and suffered from huge abandonment issues. Fear of being rejected by loved ones was something that stayed with me for most of my growing up and young adult years. I knew I never wanted to be in that position again, so I avoided a lot of personal conflict.

Even now I sometimes have to check-in with my emotions when making decisions and understand what my reasons are. But as an adult, I am wiser in my decision-making and more discerning when making them. Nonetheless, it is still a process for me, and probably will be forever.

My childhood experience left me believing that being treated badly in life by men was normal and to be expected. I allowed this to be the case as I started maturing, not realising I deserved so much more.

The sexual abuse at 9-years-old and my Father abandoning me started to take its toll. I went off the rails at school, at home and with myself. I can see how the next events in my life came so easily and how vulnerable and insecure I had become. I was desperate for love and emotionally broken.

Being rejected and abandoned by my biological Father was one of the biggest vulnerabilities I had. In addition, being sexually abused by a stranger was causing me confusion. It all became an awful time of my life and a time I wouldn't wish upon anyone. Having my Father, my hero, stripped from my life coupled with what had happened to me in Greece created my fear. I think I must have cried and cried when my Father left, I just have little memory of this time. The shock erased my memory and caused no end of butterflies in my tummy. This feeling became part of all other relationships I had with many others in my life. I believed that if someone who loved me could do that, what was stopping anyone else? I lived on a knife's edge.

High school was a very troubled time for me. I failed miserably at school, I think PE was my highest GCSE. I had been excited to go to my new school because it was close to my Father's house. But after my Father left me, I had no enthusiasm. I was a naughty child from the start. It wasn't long before I was seeing a child psychologist and labelled a juvenile delinquent. One of my school teachers met me once a week to counsel me. She listened, and I talked (or cried) for an hour each week but I don't really remember much as I was simply too afraid to really tell the truth. It was a surface conversation, but I suppose it was a little light relief if not entirely productive. My Headteacher was troubled by me, she often had me in her office during the day because I had been caught smoking on the thicket or skipping classes.

I spiralled completely out of control following the situation with my Father and into my complicated and vulnerable teenager (hormonal) years. Having been a happy child with prospects, I soon became an extremely troubled child with no focus. I was desperate to be loved and needed but was surrounded by confusion and conflicting thoughts. I couldn't see or think straight. I was terrified!

I fell quite easily into a sexually abusive relationship with an older man who, up until this point, had been someone I had trusted and someone who (looking back) had simply taken complete advantage of my vulnerability. He very carefully groomed me, became my friend and made himself my missing Father figure. He took advantage of my vulnerability. He controlled my every move. He would follow my bus to school and watch me get off and go in through the gates. He would wait for me to leave school, watch me get on the bus and follow the bus back again. He was obsessed! He manipulated me to sneak out of my parents' house in the middle of the night. He would be sat waiting just up the road with the engine switched off so as not to wake my family. He would then take me back to his house and literally drown me with alcohol and drugs, then degrade me, rape me, threaten me, sexually abuse me and scare me. I can still remember the smell of his body odour, the smell of alcohol on his breath, the smell in his car, the music he played. He laughed when he realised he had taken my virginity. I was a mess and totally knackered!

My schooling continued to suffer, and I became addicted to pain killers to numb the hangovers and headaches. I was drinking heavily, smoking, taking drugs, laxatives and became bulimic. Most days I felt more than just lost. I was out of control and had suicidal thoughts. It became a very dark time. I remember on a few occasions taking too many painkillers; I am not sure I wanted to actually kill myself, but I did want to numb the pain. This man had such control over me; he was vulgar and dangerous, and he told me not to tell anyone otherwise people would try and split us up. This man was insane! I had such low self-esteem and I allowed this to happen. Hindsight is a great thing, I can see how easy it all happened and why I didn't say anything. This was to become one of my biggest regrets in life. Not speaking out sooner.

Being groomed was easy. I was a sitting duck. I see so clearly now how it happened: lost child, abandoned by her biological Father, previous abuse, vulnerable and no self-worth - bingo! I could be shaped anyway I needed to be, so long as the attention was given to my emotional state. So, I trusted this man. I trusted no-one else, ironically, but I trusted him. It was a scary time of my life, but I have come through. And now I feel very powerful and outspoken. I want to give children, women and men a voice. I want people to understand that this behaviour is not acceptable; never has been, never will be.

When I finally realised right from wrong, I mustered up my strength to step away from him. It wasn't easy. He was everywhere I went. He showered me with gifts (leather jackets, money, diamonds, jewellery) to keep me quiet about 'our secret'. He often threatened me, would occasionally lock me in his car and travel at high speed along dangerous roads, shouting and punching the inside of the car windows. Sometimes I didn't think I would ever get out of the car alive, although some days I didn't care. I had a guilt towards this man. I didn't discuss any of this until I started my therapy, years later.

The once happy girl was now long gone. She had been replaced with a lost and broken child with no enthusiasm for anything. I was sad, lonely, scared, nervous, bulimic, anxious, depressed, tired, exhausted by my short life with no trust left at all. I felt like anything could happen to me, and I spiralled into an abyss of darkness. I was still too scared to talk and too scared to let go of the deep, dark secrets inside of me.

For many years I questioned why I let this abuse happen to me, why I didn't tell anyone?

What I have come to realise is that abusers are very good at making you feel like what is happening is ok. Even though I was scared, this is how I was made to feel. I was scared that no-one would believe me. After all, who would believe the girl who was excessively drinking and drug using, constantly playing truant, with suicidal thoughts and who was bulimic, filled with painkillers and laxatives? Or so I believed. It is almost bizarre how by not telling anyone, I allowed this to be ok. It wasn't ok. Why did I protect him or any of these people? Some people who have suffered from abuse will tell you the same. We have all ended up with a feeling of wanting to protect the bad people because of our own vulnerabilities and insecurities, as well as our fear. I was also very embarrassed - mortified actually, as well as very immature and naïve.

Also, what became even more apparent as I embarked on my therapy and new business, in my twenties, is my growing embarrassment about my seedy background, especially as I was becoming well known in my industry. I felt so ashamed that I was hiding behind my story of abandonment and abuse, not showing people who I really was. But not now. Now, I am proud of who I am and how I have got through this journey to where I am in my life today. I know how important it is to share these life stories with others and to step up and speak out.

The impact of my state of wellbeing on my loved ones, especially my mother and Stepfather, was significant. They had raised me together from when I was 3-years-old. I am eternally grateful to them both for the love and support they gave me during my turbulent growing up years. I didn't appreciate any of it at the time and I treated them both appallingly, but I now see that they never gave up on me. They only knew about the situation with my Father. I never let them close enough to find out about my abuse, which isn't unusual. I only realised this when I started my journey and by speaking with other people who had also experienced a similar incident. Like me, they buried their head in the sand in the hope that everything would go away. But as I said before, It doesn't. I know my parents were worried about me and they tried to talk to me, to understand and support me – they were despairing.

My Mother and Stepfather have been my rocks and I am very proud to be their daughter. I know they were very troubled by my life and by the world I was living in, and without knowing my full story until much later in my life, it was difficult for them. They were unable to help me because I didn't want help, I didn't understand help I just wanted to curl up and hide. I cut myself off from them for many years despite them reaching out to try to help me. I was terribly rude and horrible and had little respect or trust for them – or anyone. It was my defence mechanism. I even remember punching my Stepfather one day. And there were many occasions where I would stumble home drunk and shout abuse at my parents. I was once found at the side of the road by a policeman who recognised me and took me back home. My Mother recalls that he knocked on the front door and held me like a baby in his arms and said "Is this your daughter? We found her by the side of the road in a bush". I have no idea how or why I was there, but this is where my life ended up: alcohol and drugs. My life, up to this point was just too much for me to understand, let alone tell my parents! I used to hitchhike and behave appallingly. They assumed I had literally, 'just gone off the rails' which in fairness I had. They assumed it was due to my Father abandoning me, which of course it was too. I don't blame them for any of my misfortunes. I covered up my troubles and was an excellent actress. I dropped off from society for a good chunk of my teenage years. I felt more than lost and I battled with everyone. I wasn't a victim. I was simply in the wrong place at the wrong time. I know my parents now feel guilty, but looking back, it was not easy to detect my story at all. It wasn't their fault.

During my troubled years I would still put my Father on a pedestal even after he abandoned me. I had a romantic idea that he would come waltzing back into my life and save me. I would dream he would come back, throw his arms around me, wrap me up and hold me, then apologise and everything would be ok again. But he never came back, he never apologised, and nothing was the same again. Not in the grand gesture I had wanted. He did make vague contact over the years, but I was too troubled and couldn't cope with trying to understand any of it. I was behind my years emotionally and found myself drunk dialling him or turning up on his doorstep fuelled with alcohol and drugs. Not a good look and sadly something else he then held against me as I grew up. I was now the drunk wayward daughter, and probably it was a relief that I wasn't in his life.

I remember listening to Cliff Richard's song, *Daddy's Home* on my tape player over and over and over again, as well as watching Cilla Black's, *Surprise, Surprise* every week wishing it was me being reunited with my Father. It is interesting looking back and seeing how this affected me and how my life and emotions panned out from my childhood.

Understanding my past has given me my toughest but most educational lessons for my future happiness. I lived in a blur for so many years due to the physical and mental trauma I had gone through as a child. I could easily have dropped out of society, never achieved anything in my life or stayed in a job that didn't give me satisfaction... and for a while, I did. I suffered with a nervous disposition as a child and my vulnerabilities and insecurities as a developing young adult gave me such low self-esteem. I had little strength or control over my mind some days, and most days I was a nervous wreck, although no-one would have noticed. I took drugs and drank to overcome the mental pain. I would party hard and come home and cry. I would reach out to anyone but hide away if anyone got too close to me. I would confuse myself permanently on how best to deal with my thoughts. I was a *Grade A* mess!

The trauma of my earlier years led to a loss of memory, which I have learnt is extremely common. I have since reconnected with some of my earlier years with the help of psychotherapists, hypnotherapists plus other holistic therapists. I found Reiki had an especially positive effect on my energy levels during my recovery. The loss of my memory has been quite distressing and whilst all the treatments I have had have been hugely beneficial to my life, they were also some of the hardest sessions I have ever had to go through. Sadly, there are still parts of my memory which may have been erased forever but it is fine; I have accepted this now. It is part of who I am. What is great is that the memories I can recall are clearer and happier.

When I started my recovery I finally started to understand right from wrong. I began to understand the importance of forgiveness and I eventually let go of the bitterness and the hurt that I was holding onto. I had to rebuild my trust in my world and my life. I do understand that none of this was ever my fault. I have forgiven my perpetrators, it is their concern how they deal with their behaviour towards me. I have to let go. I really hate the word victim and have never thought of myself as one - I truly believe it was my journey to take. I have been taught very valuable lessons and have been through hoops of fire to get to where I am today. Every person's story is relative, we are all very different and we cannot judge others forever. Life really is just too short.

Having spent many years feeling like an awful person, I can now recognise that this was also part of my journey and only temporary because I had the courage and strength to step forward and seek help. Discovering the beauty within me and my passion for living has really galvanised me in both my career and personal life.

Although, flashbacks, smells, tastes, locations and music have acted as a significant reminder of the various difficult situations I have experienced, they no longer have power over me. Each time I am reminded, I take a brief moment to absorb the memory and feeling. I allow the memory to serve as a strength, reminding me of the woman I am today, which makes me very proud.

I now feel like a new leg of my journey is really beginning and I take each day as it comes. I plan accordingly and ensure my Daughter is given the best foundations that I can give her. I have found my strength and have learnt it is ok to make decisions based on how I feel.

Nowadays, if I want to do something that I wholeheartedly believe in, then I will just go for it and whatever the outcome, I will trust myself and my experiences in life to teach me a lesson! Why? Because I have developed my own self-confidence that gives me a strength to push past any fear or self-doubt. I never doubt myself or my decisions anymore and I always trust my instincts.

Having experienced being in such a lonely dark place for many years and finding my way back to myself and my life, I am now inspired to write this book and share my journey with you. Sharing my blueprint of how you can find your way back to yourself and reclaim your life is something I now feel very proud of. I have learnt so much that I want to share.

In each chapter, I share my experiences and provide you with step-by-step tools to support you on your journey to reconnect with yourself, because you do matter - never forget that.

"Are you really ready to change?"

Chapter 1
Getting Your Life Back

I remember when I was around 17 or 18-years-old, feeling absolutely broken. I felt like I must be the only one going through such a difficult time, and I really believed that no-one understood me. This wasn't surprising as I never let anyone close enough to me to find out.

I remember on one occasion getting drunk at my parents' house. I can see myself on this particular night, in the lounge and I distinctively remember that on this night, I wondered why I was even on this planet. Did I have a reason or purpose for existing? I can clearly see myself in the room having these conversations and feeling very sorry for myself. I felt totally vulnerable, overwhelmed and engulfed in low self-esteem. You could call it my *Gothic* stage. It was my way of reclaiming some semblance of control on who I was: by dressing in an alternative way and creating my own style. It felt really good.

For most of my growing years, I followed the crowd - I never thought I was that nice a person. Often, I believed that people thought badly of me. Totally crazy, maybe, but I felt completely lost. I became so paranoid about everything: walking into a room, thinking everyone was talking about me, petrified to talk to anyone about my personal life and so on. In the end, I found the only way to fit into every situation was by doing what everyone else wanted to do. Conforming seemed the only option as this covered a multitude of my problems. However, it also made it very tricky, because as I got into my late teens and early twenties, I became increasingly aware of myself. I understood so much more about my younger years and I understood that I was simply using *my crowd* as a security blanket to give me a sense of belonging.

As I started to understand the impact of what had happened to me as a child, I drank more, partied harder and took more illegal substances, something I am not proud of, yet it was the fallout from my childhood trauma. It was part of my journey and how I coped at the time until my watershed moment, which ironically, occurred in a bar I was working in.

This particular evening, one of my regulars asked me, "What do you want to do with your life?" my reply came without thought, "I would love to get back into dancing". His response stopped me in my tracks, "But you like partying too much, that'll never happen!" I felt like I'd been hit with a lightning bolt! My world stopped! It was as if there was a bright light surrounding me and I swear there were angels singing! It was such a strong and poignant moment. It was there and then I knew I didn't just want to be 'the girl behind the bar who partied a lot'. I wanted more from my world. I have since thanked this man who had this conversation with me. He doesn't remember the life-changing conversation he had. Why would he? Yet, it is something that was integral to my shift, an energy change. He had told me something that didn't enthuse me. It was as simple as this.

So, with the help of some brilliant counsellors and therapists, I started the reconnection process. With their help, support and expertise, I was gently guided back to some very difficult times in my life. I spent some time reconnecting to the younger me, the little girl who was so lost, scared, sad and confused. It was an amazing process, emotional but very powerful. I jumped back into some dark scenes in my life, replaying them and visualising my younger self in those most difficult situations. Once I could get back to a scene from my life, which wasn't always easy, I could give my younger self hope; tell her it was ok and that she no longer had to be scared anymore. I could offer her advice, tell her it wasn't her fault and give her a cuddle, reassuring her about how very much I loved her. It was such a nice feeling to give my younger self that love, attention and reassurance she so desperately needed, and it was a very cathartic and interesting journey.

Going back to some of my toughest situations and understanding the sadness surrounding me as a child was eye-opening and therapeutic. My focused psychotherapy and hypnotherapy sessions gave the young Emma-Jane lots of hope and strength. It helped me to connect. I was starting to feel like my jigsaw puzzle was being put back together, bit by bit. It really helped me overcome some of my biggest fears. I am absolutely certain I would not have been able to manage those deep sessions any earlier in my life. I would have been incapable of being so functional.

Getting Started

So now it's over to you. Are you one hundred percent ready for this journey? Are you prepared to unearth all of those locked down emotions and feelings that you might be burying very deep inside? This is your time. You need to really put time aside to acknowledge and understand who you really are.

Are you ready to consider :
- *What has happened in your life?*
- *What is it you are hiding from?*
- *What do you want from your recovery?*

You really need to want to do this. Wasting time when you are not ready could set you back. I know. For many years, I took one step forward and ten steps back, so be honest with yourself from the start. It is the only way to start this journey. You cannot cut corners or begin to think you won't have to work hard; you will work harder than you ever thought possible.

Now is the time to decide if you feel mentally strong enough to take these necessary, much needed steps to start again.

Also, never forget that your story is relative and therefore your journey will be individual to you and your life. Don't ever compare yourself with your friends and family.

It is your time to be brave. Embrace your story because we all have one.

Ask yourself:

- *What do I wish to change/resolve and what are the reasons behind wanting to change/resolve? Do I even know?*
- *Do I know what my vulnerable areas are and why I feel vulnerable here?*
- *Do I know what my fears are and how they prevent me from stepping forward?*
- *Am I ready for this?*

I like my clients to understand they will need to re-educate themselves with how they really function, both mentally and physically so they can sync themselves accordingly throughout this journey.

In short, I would like you to really open your eyes and look deep into who you are and what it is that might have deeply affected or harmed you. You might need to prepare yourself to experience those tear-jerking moments you thought you had buried away. It is time to really come alive. This is a powerful journey and one that will empower you to live your life how you need to.

When we reach our deepest, darkest moments, we cannot see how we can find the light again or the strength to even begin to live a normal life. But you can. You have to trust in yourself, be empowered by the life you have been given. We are here for such a short time. Life really is an experience and we need to make the best we can of it.

Not everything in life is straight forward or simple, but believe me, it all eventually starts to make sense when you start your soul-searching journey. Keeping your faith, taking the necessary time, however long that might be to become the you you need to be, will give you a freedom to explore what you have always wanted to do in life. Be open minded. You will most certainly be faced with emotions you didn't know you had or were capable of, but you will get there. However, you must keep the faith! Life can be wild and unpredictable, be prepared for absolutely anything and everything at any time!

"Focus on your strengths"

Chapter 2
You Can Do This!

Just because you have stopped off in life to get some help does NOT mean you are a failure. If anything, it shows you have strength and you must remind yourself of this every time you have any doubts rising within you - you are strong and stronger than you think you are.

Keep focused on finding a better life for yourself; search for yourself from within, don't give up because someone undermines what you are doing or what you are saying. Use all of this as your power to push through. Understanding your vulnerability will be one of your biggest strengths. So firstly, congratulate yourself on taking the brave steps to want a better life. Our emotional scars are our biggest strengths and when we discover and understood how to use them wisely, this will give us a happier and more fulfilled existence with much clearer emotions. Remember, *You can do this!*

I remember feeling so desperately low, confused and running scared on many occasions that I just didn't know where to turn, who to turn to or how to make things better. Some days, life seemed hopeless and other days, life seemed enjoyable.

I had a teacher at school who used to chat to me once a week at lunchtime, but as kind as she was to listen I was still very closed about what I would discuss. It did ease my emotions though, just having that outlet to cry and talk. Talking once a week was a little lid opener.

I know I spent some days feeling sad during the early days of my recovery, and whilst I don't believe I suffered from depression,

I really did know that some days were positively darker than others. I had many doubts way back at the beginning. I had no idea what my future would bring me or where I would end up. I had no motivation or plans, but as I matured I just knew I had to do something. It was apparent to me that giving myself strength was needed; I couldn't think beyond that. It took maturity and experience to turn my life around and make my days positive and happy days, which I thoroughly enjoy living now. It is how I always want to live. I guess looking back, I most likely was depressed or even suffered from *PTSD* (Post- Traumatic Stress Disorder) but having not ever gone to a doctor about my feelings and emotions for fear of what they might find out, I will never know. By nature, I am a happy person now, my troubles left their scars and have created my life today. I live a positive and happy life, but it wasn't always this way on the road to recovery. It was tough, difficult, emotional and draining. It has taken a lot for me to turn my life around to be here writing this today.

All too often peer pressure gives way to us thinking that self-help is a sign of weakness, but I can absolutely, one hundred percent say that it is not a sign of weakness. Some of the strongest people I know have had some form of therapy to support their busy lives, and still do - and "Yes", I continue to go when I feel the need to. it is ok; it is all ok. It is also good to know it is ok to not be ok during your recovery - you need to allow emotions to wash over you to develop a new power and fire.

When you have been suffering with self-doubt (for however long it might be) it really is hard to see clearly. It sometimes feels much easier to be bitter, resistant, defensive, sad and miserable. But I have learnt that it really isn't. Your energy levels hit an all-time low when you have such low self-esteem. You cannot function positively in your day-to-day life with insecurities hanging around your neck. Your work and personal life will suffer when you have lost your faith. As well as affecting your mental health, you will physically suffer because you probably won't look after your health and wellbeing. You might even deprive yourself of sleep. These are all huge factors that are triggers for depression. I was never diagnosed with depression back then or now, but as I said earlier, I suspect as a child I may well have had depression and PTSD because of the bad times I experienced. This is nothing to be ashamed of. Now, I would have no qualms in taking this to a GP, but years ago I was afraid of absolutely everything that would shift the focus onto me.

We all have busy lives and whatever you may think of therapy, it is a great tool to have in your tool box of self-help and development. We all have triggers and difficult moments in our lives and we are all capable of emotionally struggling. However, believing you can do this will help you get through the challenge you are facing. It will take some time, so investing this time in your life and recognizing that it won't be an overnight recovery will be part of building your power. Enjoy your strength and continue to be wise as you take new steps every day.

So How do You Get Out of This Dark Place?

If you are at that rock bottom moment in life, or you find you have sunk to an all-time low, then more than anything you need to find your fight, your passion for living, your love of life and motivation. We all have it, we just need to find it even when we think we have exhausted ourselves of it! It is there, within our soul. It might be as simple as picking up the phone to a friend, family or professional, or taking yourself out for a walk. It is a good start. Leaning on a trusted friend, family or professional will be a step in the right direction. You have done something for you.

What happens next is determined by your mental strength and focus. Listening to your trusted peers, maybe see a doctor if you think you are suffering from depression, and even if you aren't, a doctor can quite often be a good place to start if you are unsure of who else to turn to. Doctors (as with all professional therapists) are confidential and have your best interest at heart. I know when I started talking to professionals I was really scared about who they might speak to, but of course now I realise they are my saviours and someone to talk to. I wish I had been able to speak up sooner.

Peer pressure was one of the biggest hurdles for me. I found myself sucked in by it all. I felt I had to behave in certain ways to fit in and become part of the crowd. It is tough when you feel so vulnerable. You want people around you, but I now realise it is the right people you need around you, and what we mustn't do is allow peer pressure to get in our way of a better life. I had friendship groups at the time where I felt pressured into living the life they were living, and if I didn't participate, I would be dropped very easily, or at least that is how it felt. And that did become the truth when I decided to move away from that lifestyle. Only a certain amount of people came with me and are still with me now. I lost a lot of people from my life when I started recognising the changes that needed to happen. As I moved forward, I felt I had to fight and rise above any negativity coming from my friendship group. I consciously removed those people from my life. It takes real strength to remove people from your life who do not support your journey, particularly at the start, which is a precious and delicate time. But it is key to your recovery.

Trying to be positive during your recovery is not always easy but it really is important and key to your success. Keep telling yourself, that you can do this and find some way to feel good about yourself each day. But equally it is fine if you don't. Just keep the focus on being as positive as you can and finding a way to enjoy something of your day, you may have to dig deep to do this, and don't beat yourself up if you can't, just focus on getting up and achieving something small, maybe something as simple as getting dressed, walking the dog, making breakfast or going to work. Anything that makes you feel positive is great and will help you develop your mental and emotional state.

Fight or Flight

When we find ourselves in a situation that fills us with fear or we feel threatened by, then we most likely will find ourselves resisting (fight) or running away (flight). When you have experienced any kind of stress or trauma you will probably find you *flight* before you *fight*. I know I fought for years and didn't talk, but my flight was apparent, I would go anywhere that meant I didn't have to face up to my situations.

You may well come across days of sadness, the tears will flow and, on these days, you *will* need to dig deep and learn how to connect your sadness with the process you are going through. I eventually learnt to connect my sadness with my recovery. This is all normal and part of strengthening your resolve. I started to understand that it would eventually bring me peace and fulfilment as I went through my different stages. I learnt to surround myself with good friends who bought positivity to my life and I stepped away from those I needed to in order to keep my life moving forward with a positive focus. I talk about this more throughout the book.

You must make plans for each day, even if it is just to get up, out of bed and washing your hair. Doing anything for yourself is a positive step. Let each day give you fresh hope.

Before I go to bed each night I write a list of things I need to achieve the next day (work and personal). It gives me clarity and I feel stronger mentally when I am a step ahead of myself. It also dumps my thoughts ahead of my sleep, so I can rest easier. Some people find sleeping with a notepad by the bed a great way to brain dump during the dark hours. It was something I did in the early stages of my recovery and business.

Keep conversations with your friends and family positive and keep all your communication lines with the right people open as you navigate your way through the darkness. If you are reading this book, I hope it is because you want some inspiration on how best to turn your life around.

Remember, you can do this, and you are strong enough. Don't be hoodwinked into thinking you can't.

Life Bubble Diagram

A great tool that supported me in my recovery was creating a life bubble diagram. This helped me distinguish between the positive and negative areas surrounding my life and it can help you too. As you progress on your journey, using the diagram as a reference, you will begin to see where you are. It will also help you to develop more focus and clarity. Study the life bubble diagram below and then begin to construct your own. Take your time and make key notes.

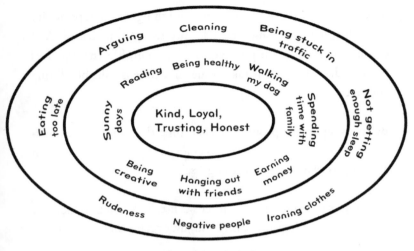

Life Bubble

As you create your own life bubble diagram, you might wish to consider the following to help you fill it out:

- *What are your strengths and talents? Write these in the inner circle.*
- *What makes you happy in life currently? Write in the middle circle.*
- *What hobbies or activities do you like? List these in the middle circle.*
- *What makes you feel anxious in life currently? Write in the outer circle*
- *Do you feel you hold the negative situations closer? Why? Add it to your outer circle.*

Having created your life bubble diagram, take time to study it. Do they balance effectively, or does the negative circle outbalance your positive circles (strengths, hobbies, happiness)? How can you flip this negativity to become much more positive? You might find you have more in your outer circle (negatives) than your inner and middle circle (positives). But do not panic. At one point in my life the negatives swamped me, but as I have moved forward I have learnt to enjoy simple activities and things to build positivity in my life, hence my middle circle (positive) has increased. As I continue to increase the positive activities in my life, the negatives become drowned out. It takes time, and time is valuable during your recovery.

By focusing on the positives and keeping the negatives at arm's-length (for now) you can start to enjoy being in the present with all that positivity and your strengths.

Looking at your hobbies and interests list, have you been actively taking part in things that bring you joy, or have they been put on hold?

Choose one that you haven't done for a while and book some time in your diary to do it, whatever it might be.

We all have strengths, but we don't always engage in them easily. You may have to dig deep to pull your strengths back to the surface of your life to start enjoying your hobbies and interests. Keeping the negativity at arm's length will allow the positivity and your strengths to integrate back into your life as they need to. Don't be afraid to ask for help either. Have a fresh pair of professional eyes look over your life bubble if you need to, but don't ignore what you have seen. Soak up the good and dismiss the bad.

"You can't fight pain with pain"

Chapter 3
Reconnecting

Looking back, I can see that reconnecting my mind and soul was by far the biggest and best start of my recovery. It was actually a relief to speak to someone, which I did in my early twenties. I had so much bottled up inside of me. I had been scared to talk and I had such a negative view of myself, of other people, everything in my life and I trusted no-one. My energy system was totally blocked, and I needed to face up to my demons before I got completely lost in a life I knew I didn't want to live.

I was more than disconnected as a child/young woman. I was emotionally dysfunctional and totally incapable of knowing what was right or wrong in relationships, and I mean in all relationships. I was immature and couldn't be close with anyone or allow anyone to be close to me. I felt like a fraud in my own life, unable to speak out or speak up. In fact, I didn't like me, and I am not sure why I would want to try and reconnect with myself?

My first ever therapy session actually started with a psychiatrist at school when I was around thirteen or fourteen years old, but I wasn't ready for it. The school had sent me to one when they believed there was no hope for me. I was labelled a juvenile delinquent. I remember seeing it on my notes when I sat with a psychiatrist in a clinical room with two chairs, a small table and a microphone sat on the table. My Mum sat outside the room. She must have been devastated! It was all really sad actually, especially now as I look back. I was never a juvenile delinquent, just a very mixed-up child. Being in that room and being asked questions I didn't know how to answer was intimidating to say the least. My heart was thumping. My school friends thought it was cool, but I didn't. I was terrified, but I was a great actress, so pretended I was cool with it all. I sat there feeling sick, shaking inside and unable to answer any questions sensibly as I was full of fear and worried I would give the wrong answer. I wasn't sure what they might have done with me. Consequently, I never talked to my psychiatrist about any of the abuse, only about my Father abandoning me. I actually feared I might go to some kind of prison.

My Bulimia also started around this time; one day I remember making myself sick, and I suddenly felt in control. I wasn't, it was just a painful part of the insecurities I was holding onto.

My journey has never stopped, but that is ok. I believe life gives us fresh challenges each day and, for this reason, I continue to discover myself daily by uncovering my potential through finding strength from others to continue reconnecting my mind and soul. Professionals are there to help us, so use them wisely. It is not a weakness to still be here, it is my strength and it continues to drive me through and give me fresh hope.

How do You Reconnect?

Can you really identify who you are and where you are in your life right now, assessing your current situation, looking at your goals and remembering where you have come from?

The process of reconnection means that you need to invest in yourself emotionally, understand and identify what is going on in your life and what has happened in your past. In doing this, it will bring you back to where you are at this very moment in your life. Consider these questions and tasks:

- *Can you clearly see your journey or understand your personal problems/issues?*

- *Can you link back to your past and understand why you have the insecurities and vulnerabilities you have?*
- *How would you rate your self-esteem levels out of 10?*
- *Do you even like yourself currently?*
- *Do you understand your trigger moments?*
- *Can you identify with your emotions?*
- *Are you able to forgive?*
- *Write down your goals (short and long term) and keep updating these as you create new goals!*

What is Low Self-Esteem?

Low self-esteem makes you feel unworthy and can make you incapable of doing anything positive. However, these feelings can only continue to make you feel like this if you don't take time for yourself to work on your mental state. The more you bury your emotions the deeper your anxiety will become. Nothing gets easier when you are in this state and it is a vulnerable time in your life.

Most of us will be very aware of what has happened to us in life, usually in our childhood, to give us the stress and anxiety we now have. However, most of us haven't dug deep enough to bring this situation or stress and turmoil to the surface, nor have we got it under our control. It is easy to cover everything up with an *invisible blanket* and hide underneath it in the hope that life will become better. But in my experience, it rarely does.

Reconnecting With Your Younger Self

One of the greatest exercises I completed during my recovery was reconnecting with my younger self. Some of my exercises were undertaken with a professional, but I was also asked to spend some time on my own going through them. If you feel happier, then maybe do this with a trusted friend or professional.

- *Sit quietly and remember one of your earliest and most painful memories.*
- *Visualise yourself as a child at that time and engage with the feeling.*
- *Once you have connected, imagine yourself with your younger self and put your arm around the mini you.*
- *Consider what you would do in this situation now and advise the younger you.*

I recall when I did this exercise, I lifted myself out of the situation and gave myself a cuddle because that is what I felt I needed to do. I then talked and advised the younger me.

This exercise takes some time. I found it really emotional. I went back to the most difficult and challenging times of my life and spent some time engaging with how I would handle this now. I didn't confront the perpetrators in each scene, I just engaged with my younger self.

Letting go of your worries, the past and the stress is a big step in the right direction. This exercise and all the exercises I did, really help to shape me and give me the strength I have today. I feel complete and strong from acknowledging and reconnecting with my most challenging experiences. I learnt early on that you cannot fight emotional pain, you can't exist with hidden anxiety and you just cannot function with painful memories. You need to let it all go. Build trust. Let it flow and let it become your journey of recovery. Don't be ashamed or embarrassed by anything you are fighting. It is part of your make-up, part of who you are. By letting it go, being honest and finding a path of peace, you will soon discover that your mind and soul begin reconnecting. I can relate feelings back to moments from my past. Letting go is quite painful, but it is a huge step to recovering. My reconnection process took quite a while to achieve and understand as I went through various therapies. Plus, it required the support of professionals.

Finding a professional(s) to talk with is a massive step and a sensible one. Remember, they don't find you, you find them. So, do your research and choose wisely.

I remember being so very scared the first time I decided to reach out to a counsellor. I felt like there was a huge stigma attached to seeing a counsellor, and I couldn't quite believe that I was going to see one. I thought I was ok, but deep down I knew wasn't. It had reached the stage where I couldn't survive any longer, so I searched and searched for the right one, not sure what, 'the right one' looks like, but I knew I needed to have a good feeling about the person I was about to open up to.

In my early days of searching, I encountered a counsellor who I never quite 'gelled' with. Deep down I knew I should never have spent any time with her, but I persevered because that is what we do when we are desperately in need of support and someone to talk to. On one occasion she fell asleep during my session. I will never forget that sinking feeling when I looked up from my tears and saw that she had nodded off. Needless to say, I didn't see her again and I reported her.

I did, eventually, find someone (after searching the phone book) who lived miles away from my hometown. I didn't want to see someone in my town. This time, I researched her thoroughly before I put in a call, which I have to say was even more terrifying! It was so scary to think that I was going to spiel off my woes to a complete stranger, especially when I had kept everything tucked safely under my *invisible blanket* for so many years; people saw me as a tower of strength. It was an alien experience but one I knew I desperately needed to do. This counselling experience changed my life, opened up my world and every little step I took gave me hope. I felt a huge relief when I left the counsellor on that first day. I got in the car, heavy with emotions and drowning in my own tears, but lighter from sharing my hidden fears and anxieties. I also learned to take a few hours out after each therapy session to allow my thoughts and heart to calm down. Going back to work straight away is never an option.

As my recovery continued, I found myself working with a mentor, which was also when my business started. Mentors can be trusted professionals, friends or colleagues who have experiences you believe would be a strength to you. My mentor is an old boss and I still check in with her when I need her guidance.

I now choose wisely when seeking support. Not only do I rely on my intuition, which gives me a good vibe when I choose someone to work with me, but also making sure that they are qualified. At the end of the book are some details about where you can search for qualified and certified professionals to support you with your recovery.

I also found writing things down very helpful. I never needed to show anyone, but I found it helpful as I pieced my life back together.

If you want to use your notes and life bubble diagram as a guide for when you start your therapy session, then do so. I found looking at my personal and professional goals (short and long term) really helpful. I could identify with my past and present and see where I needed to go. I might not have always known how to get there, but the notes were a great guide. Plus, with the help of my counsellors I could understand how best to move things forward, positively. Little steps, but nonetheless steps, and steps that were much needed.

As my journey progressed over the years I found a variety of treatments and positive sessions really helped me. I moved on with different treatments each time I felt ready to do so. My treatments included: Counselling; Reiki; Hypnotherapy; Psychotherapy; Acupuncture; Meditation; Yoga; Clairvoyance; Picture Tapping; EFT; Reflexology; Acupuncture and Cranial Sacral Therapy. I found it such a relief each time to be able to talk anonymously and let my tears flow. It was actually quite nice watching my life take shape - little steps, but positive ones too.

Such a powerful journey each time - and each time I felt stronger and ready to start the next phase of my life. Plus, during this period of reconnection and recovery, I continued to develop and strengthen my business.

When it comes to your own therapy, don't be afraid to chop and change it. Every therapist wants the best for you and it is good to experience different challenges with your therapist. I have met many and loved every one of them and all they have brought to my life.

Nothing is clear as you start your recovery journey, however reconnecting each time, will be what eventually completes you. Don't forget, that each step is a positive one. You must be patient and trust yourself, trust your journey and your recovery. This is all about you and you need to make it all about you.

Another thing that becomes really apparent during your journey to recovery is that you can't fight pain with pain, you must let it go. The only way to do this is to allow yourself to feel it. Feeling the pain allowed me to let it go and I let it wash over me. So, let the pain happen, feel it, let it wash over you and become you. This will help you understand what the pain is about and how you can manage it. I know my pain was caused by others. For years I fought my pain and avoided dealing with it. Once I accepted my pain and learnt to understand it wasn't my fault, life became kinder.

Talking became (and still is) key to my existence and key to my recovery as did surrounding myself with the right people. I still have good friends from many years ago who are very present in my life. I have also lost friends along the way, who hasn't, but no-one who I would think I couldn't be friends with again. And some friends are probably best left on the periphery. Sometimes we just have to let go of the people that are not bringing the right positivity or creativity to our life - those that can't build us up during our tough times and those that are just not around when the going gets tough. It is ok. Remember, these friends aren't bad people, they are just not right for your life, right now. It took me a while to get my head around all of this. I felt safe with friends around me, but understanding they weren't positive, good friends was hard. Letting go was like striping layers away from my confidence. I felt vulnerable.

A little word about peer pressure. Don't allow peer pressure to get in your way of a better life. Fight it, rise above the negativity and remove any people from your life (for the time being) who don't support you at this precious and delicate time. Having a strong support network around you is hugely important. You need to trust your *inner-circle* and not doubt those wanting to help you. You also need to hold at arm's length anyone who is making you feel useless and triggering your self-doubt and concern. These 'friends' don't have your best interests at heart, and the sooner you can understand this, the better. Step away. It can be hard, but it is powerful and a much-needed part of your reconnection. Be true to who you are.

All too often we get sucked into negative influences surrounding us because it is easier to follow a 'crowd' where we can hide and, to some extent, be manipulated. It might seem like an easy option. But, it isn't! It is the hardest option because it continues to cause us pain and therefore we contract into isolation, fear and despair, which doesn't allow us to truly reconnect.

If you want a stronger and happier existence, then you must fight for it. I have fought so hard and I have cried even harder. At times, I have felt like it has been the hardest journey I have ever taken. But it does all eventually make sense and one day you can look back and realise it has become the best experience you could ever have wished for. The hard days become happy days that give you a sense of completeness. You feel like you have achieved so much when you turn corners and make sense of your pain. You emerge from your cocoon.

Now, I am stronger, I have emotionally rebuilt myself with some of the best support networks I could have wished for. They have taught me to understand my past, enjoy my present and to not dwell on the future. I have been allowed to let go, to lose the bitterness I was holding on to. I have forgiven those that have hurt me and have understood how much kinder life can be when you can sleep easy at night without the burden and weight of the world on your shoulders. I have reconnected with my earlier years during each phase of my treatment and I have surrounded myself with the friends who I feel comfortable with because they are true friends.

*"Locate your power
to forgive"*

Chapter 4
Forgiveness

I know how easy it is to feel protective or guilty towards those that have hurt you. Because I felt protective towards the perpetrators in my life for a very long time.

I was very young and naïve when I was abused (emotionally & physically) and, sadly, I would've trusted anyone who showed any interest or care in me. Don't get me wrong, I had a loving family and great parents in my Mum and Stepfather, but I was trapped in a sea of darkness that no-one understood. It was totally exhausting! I didn't understand what had happened for many years. I just wanted to feel wanted and, it seemed, I was easy prey. I know I protected the wrong people for many years. Looking back, it all seems so crazy that I would want to protect anyone that would hurt me so much, but I did, and I accept that this is part of my life's journey. However, I cannot hold on to this memory. Thankfully, over the years, I have turned it all into positive energy and have created my paths to give me the strength and determination to move forward.

I now understand my error of judgement and realise why I wanted to protect these people. I believe the perpetrators drew me in to their manipulative ways. They had once made me feel safe and they had huge power over me. Consequently, this made me feel guilty about saying anything about them or about what had happened. The truth is, that once they had drawn me in and gained my trust, they took advantage of me.

It is, sadly, not unusual for anyone (children in particular) to feel protective over those that have harmed them, especially if they have been 'groomed'. Although, looking back, I feel my protection may well have been driven by fear and naivety.

It took me many years to understand the importance of forgiveness and letting go. It was a hard focus during my recovery to think I needed to forgive my perpetrators. It didn't sit comfortably with me. Why would I forgive anyone that hurt me so much? After all, they had been responsible for my damage and had stripped away my childhood. How could I forgive this? Yet, through the support of therapy and having the right people around me, I have finally let go and forgiven anyone who has hurt me - and I want you to be able to find the strength to do the same.

I am not saying this is going to be easy. It took me years to understand that my pain and vulnerabilities had been created because of my experience. I found it extremely difficult to make decisions for years because of what had happened to me with my Father. Consequently, others found it easy to emotionally manipulate me and make decisions for me. I do understand how easy it was to manipulate the girl who was emotionally broken and who was exposed to mental pain. But this is ok, I do accept this now.

I was immature and unable to process any of my insecurities, but as I matured and learnt the reality of what had happened to me, it hit me hard. After unravelling my life and processing the painful, traumatic experiences, forgiving and letting go seemed one of the most difficult things to do. I had held so tightly onto everything for so long: my deep-rooted pain and emotional insecurities. These had left me scarred by what had happened. So, for me to understand how to forgive and forget was very difficult. I had to dig deep and find that place in my heart to do so.

How do You Forgive?

You might well ask: "How do I do this?"
In my case:

- *Did the perpetrators know what they were doing to me?*
- *Did they think it was right or wrong?*

Who knows? The answer to that question is that it is their fight, not mine. I came to realise that I did no wrong as a child. I was a child. Once I accepted this, I started to grow and let go.

When the penny finally dropped, and I understood right from wrong I could eventually turn things around but not without a lot of pain, bitterness and soul searching. I cried a lot and found the long dark nights quite scary and haunting as I started to remember. Some of my memory had been shut down, and it took a long time to unlock. I doubt it will ever recover.

I had night terrors most evenings. I was a nervous wreck at the best of times. I don't know why anyone would want to hurt me in a way that no-one should ever experience. I ended up with such low self-esteem - emotionally and physically shackled. I hit rock bottom in my late teen's and was imprisoned by my world of pain due to others' selfish behaviour towards me - by adults that should have known better.

My biggest challenges were to sleep at night, to be kind, confident and to be able to love with a trust and not a broken, busted and defunct heart that prevented me from being free.

I have spent many years realising that sometimes bringing anymore fight and pain to your world is only going to get you drawn into many dark places and could potentially affect you physically, as well as lead to mental illness. I draw on the saying, "You can't fight pain, with pain." Most days, I find it a great mantra and I can allow pain to wash over me.

Losing the guilt was by far one of the hardest exercises I have experienced during my recovery. It was so difficult to fight with such enormous pain and have such huge barriers surrounding me. I blamed the perpetrators for absolutely everything. But all this did was hurt me further. I was holding on so tight to everything that I eventually developed a nervous disposition and felt permanently nauseous at school, I took laxatives and became bulimic. I was a nervous wreck during my schooling and my concentration in classes went out of the window. I rebelled and did all the things I shouldn't do just to survive my school years. I am not proud of this, yet I also now recognise that it was my survival instincts.

I can honestly say that I now hold no bitterness towards anyone anymore and wish everyone the best success in their lives and futures. I have let go of the pain and understood that my life is much richer because of this. I am NOT grateful or proud of what I had to endure to be here, but I have made it a positive lesson to help others and give those that need it, a voice.

I have forgiven my perpetrators for what they did to me, but I can NEVER condone what they did to me. This was a sick act of cruelty to a child, and totally unacceptable. But to let go, I have had to understand that my perpetrators have problems they need to work on, and their problems aren't mine to carry. This doesn't make it right, but their feelings and emotions are not my responsibility and I have to accept this. None of this was my fault. I was simply in the wrong place at the wrong time with the wrong people, just as many others have found themselves in.

How do we Stop Any of This From Happening?

We keep speaking out and finding our voice to give others confidence, especially children. The more we raise the subject the easier it is for others to hear.

So, do You Recognise Your Emotions of Guilt And Pain?

It really is vital you spend time on who you are and where you want to be in your life. From this position, you can really look at what has gone on a little bit more objectively, albeit, still an emotional exercise. By discovering and reconnecting with the person you have lost sight of during your troubled times, you can really help find those building blocks back to who you really are and uncover your potential and magnificence.

If you refer to the life bubble you constructed from chapter 2, you can use it to help you reconnect with who you are, now. Focus again on what your strengths are and how your positives can bring you clarity. Drive the negative situations away and learn how to flip them to become positive energies in your life. For example, I used to be fearful and worried about so many things, such as walking into a room on my own and speaking my truth. Through reconnecting with who I am now, I can walk into a room on my own without feeling like the ground is going to swallow me up and I can stand up and say how I feel without feeling ridiculed.

By releasing the guilt towards those causing you pain or those you might be protecting, you will learn a valuable lesson in moving forward and strengthening your mind. I was scared to speak out for many years as I was just too worried that I might upset my perpetrators.

On your journey to recovery, you might end up feeling bitter and have haunting nightmares, which is not unusual. This whole process of reconnecting with yourself means you must literally turn yourself inside out, which can leave you wide open and exposed to a whole new world of vulnerability. Essentially, this is why it is important to stay close to the positive aspects and strengths of your life.

When you start finding your inner strength you will find it easier to move through those difficult times and, as scary as it may seem, it really will be the right path to follow, trust me. You will eventually learn to let go of the bitterness and move away emotionally from your perpetrators and be confident in speaking out. It might have taken me 35-years to speak up, but I eventually got there. Now, people listen to my story about how my life has changed.

Coming to terms with what has happened, however painful, becomes a strong motivational force that will bring so much to your future life. It might not feel like it at the time but, trust me, once you can openly speak about things (whether it be in a counselling session or telling your family or in a professional situation) you will gain a lot of inner strength.

When I sat my parents down to discuss what had happened to me, they were horrified and naturally blamed themselves. But how were they to know? It wasn't their fault. I don't blame them at all and I have told them that. I spoke to a few friends over the latter years. However, I was very scared about sharing too much and, often, I actually did not know what to say.

Forgiving your perpetrators will be a double-edged sword. But eventually you will learn that it really will be a great strength as you move forward. It will allow you the freedom to handle any negativity and give you a fresh approach to your next phase. Letting go will bring you a level of calm. Stepping back will allow you to see things clearly and forgiving will allow you to move on as you accept you can't live other people's mistakes. I have found a calmness within me towards each perpetrator that I have forgiven; it doesn't make what they did right, but it helps me to let go.

Talking your story through with a professional is by far the most focused way forward, to start with. I also found that writing down my feelings towards each of my situations was a great way to link everything back together, which helped me piece my life together. I could see it for what it was, and I could understand my error of judgement with a greater clarity.

Learn to Forgive

Learning to forgive can be challenging and is often misunderstood. It doesn't excuse the behaviour of your perpetrators, and neither is it about forgetting the events either. Forgiving is more about acceptance. An acceptance that you have experienced these events in your life. Up until now, these events have influenced how you relate to others and yourself. It is now time to release this influence and release your limited view of yourself and your world. Expand your pathway towards the life you want and remember that you have done nothing wrong. Tap into your unlimited potential and set yourself free.

Find the strength to dig deep and release yourself from the pain. No-one controls your thoughts more than you do and it is important to grab your reins. However painful.

Throughout this book, I have focused on sharing my experience and offered guidance which supported me on my journey to recovery. I know how hard it is to forgive and it can be a long journey. I one day decided to forgive my perpetrators for what they did as explained in this chapter. I now see their selfish needs were not personal to me. I am sure that I wasn't the only girl to have suffered from their hands, and it is something I hope others realise too; they are not personally responsible for the acts committed against them. Rather, these perpetrators seek out and target those they deem vulnerable - in my case, a vulnerable child.

I sincerely hope that in reading this book and taking this journey, you will regain your confidence and self-belief, as well as use the tools that helped me to prevent long-term mental and emotional damage.

"Are those around you strong enough for your journey?"

Chapter 5
Ring-Fence Your Life

Relationships became a huge problem for me. I had a fear of men and women, ironic now, but I did. I had zero trust in anyone, even my close friends. I had this insecurity surrounding me that gave way to me feeling vulnerable in everyone's company. I couldn't see the good from the bad at times, and I didn't know how to see the good from the bad either because I had such low self-esteem. It was so confusing and complicated.

During my recovery, it was essential that I kept the focus on me and not others. And now I share that with my clients. Focus on you. Life will play out as it needs and fall into place where it needs to, but don't get distracted from who you are and where you are.

Having a strong support network around you is hugely important. You need to trust your "inner" circle and not have any doubts about them. At the same time, you also need to learn how to hold at arm's length those "friends" and situations that make you feel useless or amplify your self-doubt and concern.

For many years I hung out with friends who wanted to party, which was a great way to hide behind my insecurities. They were fun nights out but sadly not always happy nights for me. I would get so drunk and then go home and cry my eyes out before I passed out. Or, I would get so drunk that I would pass out and be carried home. Regardless of which option I chose, it was always painful. This way of existing for me was just another day that had passed and another day away from the trauma. Blotting out the past seemed so much easier for me than confronting my problems. I didn't know how to confront anything.

Understanding who and what I needed close to me was quite a difficult part of my journey. I was surrounded by lots of people, people I really enjoyed being with and people who I thought I trusted. But when I started to break it down I soon realised who was who, and who wasn't right for my life during my recovery. They weren't bad people. They just weren't right for where I was in life. This wasn't their fault, it was just a process. I am friendly with everyone, even now, but I am much more cautious about who I let in.

Do You Know Where You Fit Into Your Life?

When I started my recovery I also stopped drinking and naturally my social life changed also. Instead of partying, I focused on my business and I started my therapy. During this change in my life, my circle of friends changed too. Was I surprised? Not really, well maybe a little. But I had no real feeling towards this at the time. Neither am I judging anyone in my life, I just moved on and took the friends I needed with me. I stopped working in bars and restaurants and took myself out of situations that were causing me harm.

By identifying which friends benefit you and your life, you will start to gain a clearer perspective on who you need near you. I found as I stepped away from a life that was holding me back, I introduced myself to new friends who I felt comfortable with. I opened up my world to some truly beautiful people that I felt I could trust and who could enhance my life, and vice versa. My friends became hugely diverse and, at this present point in my life, I feel blessed by my circle. Some have been with me since I started my new journey, and some have come in more recently. I know if I needed, I could now really ring fence my life with a power of strength; something that has taken me a long time to feel confident about. I can also step back and look at my situation clearly and with a wise head. This, I realise, comes with awareness and is a good tool to have in your recovery tool box.

Identifying the people that you can take with you on your next journey is a difficult process, but one that will give you moral and trusted strength at a time when you need it. You know yourself who you need to keep close and those who you need to hold at arm's length. Focus on what you really want to do when you start your journey of recovery and be confident with stepping forward to make your changes. You will soon understand who is with you and who isn't.

Find new hobbies or projects to participate in. Be open-minded when meeting new people. You will be surprised at how your life expands as a consequence. It will give you fresh hope at a time when you really need it. For me, I went back to dancing and exercise. Two things I loved and that made me happy and, of course, formed two of my businesses.

It is also very important to be comfortable in your own company. However, anyone who has been abused knows how difficult it can be to be on your own. I know I struggled for years to be alone. I would often make sure someone was always with me. I am much more content in my own company these days, and I will happily sit at the Spa enjoying my own company, spend a day out shopping, or even sip a cup of mint tea at the coffee shop. It is healthy to be able to do this. Equally, I am just as happy when I am surrounded with friends, family and my Daughter. Although, I still actually prefer to be with people, however, I can be on my own too. Nothing pleases me more than taking my dog for a nice long walk on my own.

Depression – The Silent Killer

It can be dangerous to be on your own without professional support or without finding some positive energy when you are going through dark times. Depression is a silent killer and must not be ignored by anyone. In this case the abused, depressed person will maybe want to be on their own. This is when friends and family must recognise symptoms and gather their strength to help loved ones through these difficult times and not let them isolate themselves. Being with others, talking and being active will allow you to find the path of strength to recover. You do not need to be isolated. As a young child, I wanted to be on my own many times and wallowed in self-pity.

Suicide from depression is a leading cause of death in the UK. I have spent a lot of time promoting the importance of mental health through my various media platforms. There is no stigma attached, it needs to stop being a taboo subject, as it is an area that we seriously need to address. Helping others suffering gives hope. Firstly, listening to those suffering with depression, is vital. Friends and family should listen without advising – I know family who tried to advise me, but you can't take advise really from immediate family, it is too close. However, encouraging the person suffering with depression to seek professional help is a great way to support as is accompanying them if they feel nervous (although you probably won't be allowed in the session, you can wait outside.)

It is also important to understand some depressions or those suffering with bipolar need a lot more support than talking therapy. Recognising depression is difficult, so it is wise to speak to a GP if in doubt. There are great websites around if you have any questions you need answering, either for yourself or friends.

You can take a look at the following for support www.mind.org, www.samaritans.org, www.rethink.org, to start off with.

All too often we get sucked into negative influences surrounding us because we are programmed by society and find it easier to follow the crowd. We hide, we can be manipulated and we find it a much easier option to crawl underneath our *invisible blankets*. But this is the hardest option, NEVER the easiest. It continues to give us pain and suffocates us into isolation, fear and despair. Hiding behind anything or anyone gives us a false sense of security and gets us nowhere fast in sorting out our problems. Stepping away from your veil of fear will give you the strength you need to find a way forward, even if it is just picking up the phone to a friend, GP or counsellor. You can do it! Trust me. I never thought I could, but I did. I found the strength to push forward in my life and find the power to make changes by including the right people in my circle of trust. Now I have a greater sense of clarity and understand the veil of fear that covered my life for many years.

Healthy Boundaries

It is important for you to create healthy boundaries on your road to recovery. Your self-care is the most important thing, as are the people you allow into your life.

Ask yourself these questions, then go back to your life bubble diagram and add to it based on your answers:

- *Are you able to distinguish between those you need close in your life right now? Write down who keeps you positive in the middle circle of your life bubble.*
- *If anyone makes you feel slightly awkward or anxious, are you comfortable about putting them in your outer circle and holding*

> *these people at arm's length at this point of your life? You can also create your own friends' bubble and see clearly who should be kept close and who shouldn't, at this moment in time. Understand what these friends bring to your life.*

- *Aside from friends, what else can you hold closer to your life right now? Work/Hobbies/Family.*
- *If you find family are drawing on your emotions, then it is fine to hold them at arm's length too. It is not forever. It is until you can emotionally know how best to cope. Don't feel bad about putting them in your negative, outer circle. It is all part of your journey.*
- *Do you know where your happy place is? Write this in the inner circle of your life bubble.*
- *What are your weaknesses'? You know your strengths, now on the outer circle write your weaknesses' and build your picture.*

Your life bubble will be taking shape as you can really start seeing what drives you, what holds you back and what motivates and inspires you.

"Allow your fear to guide you back"

Chapter 6
On the Other Side of Fear

Fear. What is it? The online dictionary defines it as *'an unpleasant emotion caused by the threat of danger, pain, or harm'* and is to *'be afraid of someone or something as likely to be dangerous, painful, or harmful'*.

I've faced fear head on. I've seen the anguish it brought to my life, the barriers it put up around me, the emotional pain it caused and the physical stress it had on me. Fear was my daily companion as a result of my traumatic experiences, and I hid behind that fear for many years. This only resulted in an escalation of feeling fearful. Yet, I held on to my fear like a security blanket; it had become so familiar to me and I was not emotionally equipped to know or understand how to manage my fear. It didn't seem fair, yet in that time and space, it was the only way I knew to respond.

I was terrified of the consequences of letting go of my fear. I truly believed that because the fear had caused me so much mental and physical damage that to let it go would only potentially tip me over the edge, it would raise questions I didn't know how to answer - part of me felt it was all my fault anyway. I felt like a victim some days. I felt responsible for the gut-wrenching pain I felt, and I truly believed I deserved it.

It has been a valuable lesson to my life as I have recovered. Whilst a tough lesson that I might not have originally wanted, I am also strangely glad I have had this opportunity to explore my fear. I can look back now with an open mind and see the trail of disaster I left behind me. I understand it was part of my journey.

As a young girl growing up into my world (life/business/ Motherhood) I was controlled each day by my routines and plans. I had a mild case of OCD as a young adult which I overcame after gaining control, yet fear created other control issues within me. We can't hide behind fear. Eventually, the consequences become huge. Not only does your life get physically wrecked, you end up mentally unstable too.

From confronting my fears over twenty years ago, I can now safely and securely manage my emotions with positive therapy, and by looking forward, not backward anymore. If I am faced with fear, I jump into it and enjoy the exhilaration I get from doing so. I have finally made friends with fear, as it has helped me to find my own personal power and integrity, as well as to trust in my ability to find solutions to the challenges in my life.

What I have found truly amazing over the last 35 years or so, is how feeling out of control impacted me emotionally and physically with conditions such as: Bulimia, OCD, drinking, drugs and behavioural problems. There is a direct link. It is much more noticeable these days and acted upon, but there is still an issue getting others to accept that behaviour problems have a past. As I recovered my strength and battened down the hatches, the bad habits were blown out of the water and dispersed.

My fears were banished by my focused therapy sessions and took a long time to overcome. I found fear at every corner and at every twist and turn. I was overwhelmed at nearly every situation I faced and handled it all badly. Facing up to my fear turned so much around for me. It was not easy but learning from my mistakes was a good way to start overcoming my fear. Every day I learnt more, and I got stronger, more durable and able.

Finding Your Strength Through Fear

Do we fear change more than we fear the things in our life that cause us anguish? I think it is a valid point and one that works in relation to our life. Confronting our fear is a fear in itself, and once overcome, our fear of change is no longer an obstacle. Plus, we can use our newfound confidence to fight the anxieties causing our challenges.

So, how do you confront your fear?

- *Consider, what it is that is holding you back and scaring you? Be brutally honest. It will be a hard exercise to complete, but it will be a lifechanging moment. Write it all down in the outer circle of your life bubble.*
- *Take your fear list and talk it through with someone else, such as a friend, professional or visit your GP. Don't be embarrassed. You have done nothing wrong.*
- *Talking therapy with a trusted person is a great part of recovery and a great way to heal and understand. All fears can pretty much be linked back to your past. They will have matured like an emotional fertilizer that you have fed yourself over time through your self-doubt.*

Imposter Syndrome

Imposter Syndrome is a psychological pattern that causes doubt. You don't feel adequate to perform even though you are highly qualified to do so. You feel a hidden failure and hide away covering up your fear, for fear of being exposed.

I learnt about Imposter Syndrome during the latter part of my journey. After researching this phenomenon, I was actually relieved to know I had it. Because after years of riding my wave of recovery I was still not sitting comfortably until 5 years ago. I could now put a name to my fear of standing up and being heard. I realised that I had been hiding behind myself as I progressed in my business and my personal life. On the surface, I was showing I was a tower of strength, but deep behind that I had a few butterflies still. My fear of speaking up honestly about who I was, was great. I was working very hard with everything in life to improve who I was, improve my business and my personal life...but I was still not settled. I was terrified of anyone finding out about my life - that I had been a boozer, drug user and a gold star nervous wreck in my youth. I had done nothing wrong, but I had a fear of my childhood being exposed. How would that come across to my clients, my platforms and my new friends? I was living in fear, despite achieving so much, and as I was interviewing guests on the sofa for my *Wellbeing Show* with *That's TV* each week, I felt a fraud.

I was all over social media, all over the internet and all over the UK sharing my brand, telling people who I was, what my businesses were and how I could change lives. I was confident in my lessons in life and how I could help others in business and their personal life. And I was especially confident in how I could continue to shape my world and my business. But something was still holding me back. I had started writing my book in earnest at the back end of 2016 and nervous as I was, I wanted to put it down on paper.

My Stepfather told me early on in life that knowing what he knew now, he wished he had taken more gambles in life. He also used to say, if it goes wrong then so be it, just pick yourself up and find another way round the situation. Two strong pieces of advice. I used these words throughout my business and personal life to help me overcome my fear and each time I stepped through, I found it was ok. I pushed my boundaries and found my confidence. I am now me. I have been pieced back together and my life is feeling complete. I have found my platform and confronted so many of my fears.

Naturally, as I continue in business I am faced with new challenges. It is up to me to work out how to deal with them, learn from them and understand what they can bring to my life and my future. I choose wisely regarding business situations and projects, considering whether I can handle them. And I always weigh up how productive they are professionally and emotionally.

So, when it comes to fear, ask yourself:

- *Are you in control of your life?*
- *Who do you want to be and where do you want to be right now – personally and professionally?*
- *Are you in touch with your emotions and do you understand your emotional responses?*
- *Are you truly reflecting the person you wish to be known as or are you hiding behind yourself, for fear of being exposed?*
- *Do you understand your strengths and weaknesses?*
- *Where do you see yourself heading in life personally or in your career?*
- *Write your future plans in the middle circle of your life bubble.*
- *Do you think you have Imposter Syndrome?*

There are number of articles on the internet that describe Imposter Syndrome, which you might find useful. Simply type in Imposter Syndrome in the search engine to find them.

Unmasking Fear

- Using your FEAR to drive you will give you more confidence than you ever could have imagined. So what if it doesn't turn out as you wanted? That's called a lesson and lessons are part of our education and an opportunity to improve.

- Another way to look at FEAR, is through the acronym: False Evidence Appearing Real, which is sometimes what your FEAR is based on. So, it is important to discern whether your fear is based on facts or your mind. Through this discernment, you will start discovering the real you. You will also find new ways and energy to create a better life, carving out a future that will be fuller and richer in more ways than money.

- Allow your vulnerable side to drive your passion; the side that holds your enthusiasm and zest for life. Make decisions that give you excitement and allow you to work with a focused mind.

- Being you, truly you, will give you a drive and determination that is real, raw and driven by passion and enthusiasm. Let go and see what happens!

- Who is stopping you?

*"What does your voice
want you to say?"*

Chapter 7
Finding Your Voice

My favourite chapter. Finding your voice.

I have been in business for over 20 years, and during this time I have spoken at many events, given presentations and offered advice and support within my working arena. I felt safe giving these presentations because the focus was on a product, topic or client and not about me. For a long time before I spoke up and out, I was settled in my life, confident with where I had got to, and pleased with my progress in life both professionally and personally. I actually never wanted to share my story, but as time went on, I felt this growing desire to share my experience - more so when I started working for Oxfordshire's *That's TV* as the presenter for *The Wellbeing Show*. I began to recognise that I had a platform which could give me the power to help others. Also, I was interviewing people with very brave stories to share and I sat there feeling a fraud.

Imposter Syndrome was riddled all over me and as I progressed with my media work, and my name became more well-known locally, it made me feel rubbish, questioning who I was and where I had come from. Interviewing real people, brave enough to share, made me realise that I was sitting behind my mask to hide my history. In short, I sat there with everyone looking at me, the girl who had the perfect life, but behind all of that I was the girl who had worked hard to have the perfect life.

I wanted to be heard and respected for my business, which I was. I was recognised for the work that I did – no-one aware of my life story - and this was really important to me. It was never a sympathy acceptance, which I would never have wanted. I just wanted to be respected for what I had achieved in life. I knew the achievement was huge in so many ways. From the humble beginnings of my career - a fragile girl, looking for little ways to make it back into life, doing something I enjoyed. It was called survival. I was looking to be validated constantly and finding reasons to be validated. I believed that people only liked me for what I had achieved rather than just liking me for myself. I really didn't understand that being validated was not important, and as I started to become wise to my life I realised this was important to resolve.

Giving my clients their voice back is one of the biggest hurdles to overcome during any stage of recovery. It is not just to be listened to, but to be heard and seen, fully expressing themselves and their truth. I have been at many presentations where the speaker is talking and being listened to, but you can see no-one is actually hearing or seeing the speaker because they have failed to connect with their audience. Instead of listening, the audience have switched off, checking their phones, reading notes and frequenting the bathroom. It takes a special person to step up, speak up and be heard by their audience.

The first time I spoke about my story, I was at the *Media Hub* in Cookham. There were around 25-30 people in the room. The organiser had started to learn of my story, and my intentions of writing my book, so she kindly offered me a few minutes of the evening to speak. Nerve racking stuff. I wrote my 4 minute presentation and bullet pointed my story. It was real and heartfelt. When I stood up to speak I wanted the world to swallow me up, but I knew I had to do this - this was my time, and this was my opportunity to push forward. So, I started, and the room fell silent. You could have literally heard a pin drop. I jumped through my fear and found a new strength. A few women contacted me afterwards to thank me for sharing my story as it had inspired them to look at their past. As I said at the beginning, my story is relative. Everyone has a past and my story is not (sadly) uncommon. I have since heard from lots of women who relate to my story.

After the *Media Hub* evening, I spoke at The *Venus Women Awards*. Another step. A bigger step. I was approached by the *Venus Women Awards* committee to stand up and be counted as a woman in business. They were going to do a feature on my work, my life and they gave me a 6-page spread in their summer magazine. On top of this, I was then asked to compere at their summer award ceremony. This would mean my life would also be on the big screen at the event, recognising me as a woman in business in front of 250 guests.

It hit me right between the eyes! There and then, I knew this was my moment, my final moment of fear – a fear of exposure! I knew that I could use this opportunity to stand up and tell my story, or I could just do what I had been doing up to that point and share what I wanted to keep my life simple. Simple isn't part of my nature. I saw this as my opportunity to put my life out there and stand up, be heard and give my voice its first sincere airing about who I was to the business community. I worried it might be a car crash for my career, but I knew I had to do this. It wasn't the small audience I may have preferred for my disclosure, instead, it was into the deep end! Since that defining moment, I have not looked back. In taking a risk to speak up, I overcame my fear and gained respect for my authenticity and willingness to share my story.

This was a huge step forward, I was now speaking in front of around 250 people. Plus, my story was on video on the big screens before I entered the room, displayed around the venue where the awards were. It was part of the magazine story I had done previously, which touched on my personal life and offered a hint of what was to come. Speaking at this event was terrifying! I shook. I stopped half way through and asked the room to give me a minute; after this I finished with ease. I felt such pride and respect for myself for this achievement. I had succeeded! My voice was getting stronger and I had found my fear to be my strength.

Finding Your Voice

I want you to feel this journey gives you the freedom to step up, step out and be heard for what you need to be heard for. Allow yourself the freedom to speak your truth. I have a platform that I have worked hard to create, I have gained the respect of others, and finally found my own self-respect. Respecting yourself is so important. Do you respect yourself for what you have achieved or what you are doing in your life?

Not everyone wants to stand in front of 250 people and speak, some of you might just like to have the confidence to ask your neighbour for a cup of sugar because you have run out, but whatever it is, it is ok. You can speak up and ask for the sugar or stand in front of a 250 strong audience. You have the ability to be heard, do you know that?

Being respected for who you are, what you do and what you stand for is hugely important in life. Everyone can command respect, it doesn't matter who you are, someone somewhere will have respect for you. Do you know what that respect might be for you? Think about what you bring to your life, to others and the value you add to other people's lives.

Do you have friends or family that you enjoy speaking to, or are you the type of person who really doesn't have anyone? Why is that? Do you feel lonely or are you drifting from location to location?

Whatever it is, someone somewhere is on your side and respects you. They want to hear from you and they want to listen to you. Whether it is sat in a park talking about life, or in a boardroom sharing your professional views. You are respected and with respect you have a voice. You just may not know how to use it yet. How would you like to use your voice?

Create a voice bubble diagram to discover how much you have to share. Draw your diagram, using the image below as a guide. Focus on what you can share to inspire others, whatever it is. You don't have to share this diagram with anyone.

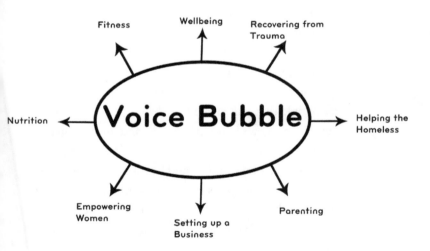

When finding your voice, it is important to understand what you are trying to achieve in your personal and professional life. What are your goals and also what are your blocks to achieving those goals? Once you can start growing personally and professionally, you will find your motivation for living the life you want.

1. Write a list of professional goals and a list of personal goals. Things you really (and realistically) can achieve in your lifetime.

2. Next understand what you need to do to achieve your personal and professional goals. For example, one of my early goals was that I wanted to return to dancing and one of my personal goals was that I wanted to stop drinking. So, to do this I moved away from that life I was living and began temping to earn some money. Then I started a tap class for beginners and stepped back from the drinking circle of friends. I made new friends and although an untrusting soul, I began a calmer journey that filled me with happiness. My goals grew, my ambitions grew and my confidence grew. Little acorns. I made new friends and created a new life for myself.

3. Keep up to date with your goals and check in every few months on where you are with them. Log it all in the middle circle of your life bubble that you created in chapter 2. I continually check in on my goals both personally and professionally. I have grown in every way since I started my business and because of this I can now understand how I can use my voice. One of my professional goals now is to continue developing my work, globally. There I have said it. It is out there and one of my personal goals is to continue spending valuable time with my loved ones.

What stops you from speaking up and out? Is it the fear of not being heard or the fear that you haven't got anything interesting to say? One of the most interesting statistics is that public speaking is the number one fear among us. But I also believe that many of us have a fear of what others might think about us. You might have to dig deep, but rest assured, you are absolutely capable of speaking out. Like I said earlier it could be to a friend or in front of a 250 crowd - you can do it and having confidence will help you.

Having been on this journey of reconnection, I now feel truly confident and comfortable with myself. I am respected, and people can relate to me. I absolutely have a strong belief in who I am and what I can do to support others in life, I don't doubt who I am, and I constantly educate myself and talk to others in my life to develop my strengths. This serves to support me in developing my qualities, which enriches my life and my personal and professional networks. I have discovered and uncovered this valuable lesson through my journey; it isn't driven into to us as kids and maybe it should be, maybe we should be educated on the benefits of being mentally fit and well? As a parent, I spend a lot of time talking with my Daughter on this subject matter.

Assessing Your Confidence

This is an area that we often don't like to look too deeply at, we'd rather throw our *invisible blanket* over the whole thing. However, being honest with yourself will benefit you and your journey toward speaking up and speaking out.

Ask yourself the following questions:

- *Do you have confidence in life? What does having confidence actually mean to you?*
- *What do you fear about speaking out?*
- *Knowing your strengths and weaknesses, will allow you to build a picture of who you are.*

- *Write at the bottom of your life bubble page what you feel confident at doing and being?*
- *Your life bubble should be starting to take a good shape now. Can you see things more clearly when you look at your life on paper?*

*"Can you see beyond
your reflection?"*

Chapter 8
Who Are You?

Who do you see when you look in your mirror? What do you want to see? Is your reflection a true image of who you are and where you are in life?

We all look in a mirror every day, but do we really look at ourselves or do we just take a glance? Is it more cosmetic when you see yourself in your reflection? What do you really see or, more importantly, who do you really see? Next time you look in your mirror, see if you register your reflection. Do you recognise the person looking back at you in the mirror? Does that person resemble who you really are, or have you lost sight of yourself so much that you can't see yourself clearly?

I discovered the mirror early on in my recovery and found that by really looking at myself and registering my reflection, I could see the person I hadn't seen for a long time and I learnt how to love the person looking back at me. People could not see my wounds, my broken heart or my shattered mental state because physically I hadn't changed, or had I? I think I looked older back then – I certainly felt it. My skin was sunken, grey, drawn and exhausted. The years of being bulimic, drinking and drug use took its toll. I could clearly see the damage done. I didn't like my reflection. In fact, I hated it! I hated what I saw and who I had become. I just couldn't see a way out. I hated me. It is hard to believe now, but I really did.

Each day we get up, get dressed, do our hair (make-up) brush our teeth and look in a mirror to assess our visual image - we are conditioned to do all of this. However, we never really take a good look. We see our reflection as cosmetic, but we never really look deep enough at the person staring back at us, and, to be quite honest, why would we? We haven't been conditioned to do so, therefore it doesn't seem natural to us; it is simply a mirror doing its job, which is ensuring we look the way we need to before we start our day, right?

But if you look closer (and this is the hard bit) you can really start to identify with the person staring back at you. You can learn more about yourself in a 5-minute session looking in the mirror than you would ever have imagined. The mirror is a great way to take a step back and study yourself, to find out who you are. You can give yourself time to speak, question yourself and discover who you are. You have been living a long time. Have you registered the change in your reflection over this time or just accepted it? Most of us accept this because we can't physically do anything to change it. But, I believe that we actually can. Emotional and mental fitness can bring about a physical change in our very being. Studying your reflection can give you great clarification.

Can you match the person in the mirror with the person standing the other side? I can now, but I never could before.

Mirror Exercise

When you start this exercise make sure you have time on your hands to explore your reflection. This could be a difficult task depending on where you are with your recovery. You will need a mirror, good lighting, a notepad and time. Don't rush this exercise, just take your time and consider the following questions:

1. First, take a good look at your face, your features and look at how your face has physically changed. Is your reflection

reflective of your emotions? Do you feel any strength or confidence? What do you see from the person staring back at you?

2. Do you recognise yourself from the baby/toddler pictures? I can really remember one or two pictures of myself as a child. I can relate to the innocence and honesty that life gave me back then. What do you see?

3. Are you happy with the person looking back at you? I know I found it difficult to align myself with my reflection during my recovery. It really was troublesome for me. I saw such pain and such innocence. Yet such difficult times and such maturity from a life I had no choice but to find.

4. What has happened to you in your life? Talk to yourself about your experiences. You might feel awkward about this to begin with but do persevere. Start by asking yourself how you feel about the challenges you've experienced in your life? Consider how these past or present challenges are holding you back. It is also good to look at the positive happy times too, especially relating to challenges you have overcome. See how your face changes each time you speak. Can you see the range of emotions in your face during your conversation? We talk so much to other people, why should it not be ok to speak to ourselves?

5. What are your eyes saying? Eyes can say so much. The saying, 'she smiles with her eyes' is so true. Do you? For years, I saw darkness in my eyes; I felt the darkness and I could barely look at my eyes. I didn't want to acknowledge the pain staring back at me. I didn't know what to do with it or how to change it, so I avoided eye contact with everyone, including myself.

6. Are you smiling because you are happy or out of habit? Smiling is so important in our day-to-day lives. If you smile, the world smiles with you. It is true. It really does. How much do you smile in your day? When you smile how do you feel? I work in the media and do a lot of public events, so my smile is part of my business. These days it is a genuine smile, but it never used to be. It used to be fake and full of fear. Now it is open and full of energy. Of course, I get the days I don't feel like smiling but that is normal. You can't fight pain with pain, so I ride this wave in a positive manner. I think my smile is prettier now than it was back then.

7. Now consider whether your reflection is true to you? Is how you feel inside reflected in the mirror? This is tough and a big question to ask yourself. Are you looking at who you want to be? Are you happy to see yourself staring back, knowing what you know about yourself? Answer truthfully.

Once you have completed this part of the mirror exercise, you will need your notepad to write down 5 things about your reflection. Try to be as observant as you can be:

1. What colour is your hair? Is it long/short/receding? Do you like the style? Could you change it? Have you wanted to change it? What would you do with your hair to make you feel happy?

2. What colour are your eyes? Are they looking tired, blood shot, aged? What shape are they?

3. Is your face round, oval, square, diamond, heart, rectangle, oblong, pear? Do you compliment your face by wearing the right clothes/hair/make-up, or do you just get dressed

and put on the same creams/make-up? Do you ever go out without make-up?

4. Have you ever noticed what shape your body is? Are you an apple or a pear? Does your body look fit and toned or tired and puffy? What do you want it to look like? How does it make you feel looking back at your shape?

5. Do you slouch or are you standing tall? Posture is so important to our lives. You might not have even thought about your posture, why would you? But sitting correctly and standing tall all helps during your recovery. It also keeps you mentally aware of your physical appearance. Before you read this, consider how you were sitting before. Has it changed after reading this?

Once you have noted the 5 things about your reflection, write 5 things about you as a person:

1. Do you like how you physically look? If you've answered in the negative, then what could you change so you feel more positive about your physical appearance? If you feel positive about how you look, then write down what you like about your reflection? Be brutally honest with yourself. Write it all down on your paper - get it all out there and available for you to see it.

2. What do you like about you as a person? How would you describe yourself? Again, you need to be brutally honest. I remember my list being very limited.

3. What would your friends and family like about you? What do you think they would say about you if they had to describe you physically?

4. Which part of your body don't you like? Most of us will have a part of our body that we struggle with. Learn to love the bits you don't like by accepting they are part of who you are. Without them, you wouldn't be you.

5. If you could change one thing about your physical appearance what would it be and why? Once you have acknowledged what it is, you can start doing some work with yourself and your therapist on this part of you. It might not be something you thought of as important, but it is. Learning to love how you look helps to bring you back in alignment with yourself. Recognising that everyone is unique and different is something for celebration. So, fall in love with your uniqueness.

The reflection exercise can really help you understand the type of person you are outwardly. It can also give you an insight into what other people see. It is true that if we feel better we act better and whilst this book is all about working from within, it is also good to layer this up with your outward appearance too. Syncing your mind and body is a very good step to getting you back in line with your mental and physical wellbeing.

I can now look in my mirror and be brutally honest about who is staring back at me. I like who I am emotionally and mentally, but occasionally I can be critical about what I physically see, and this exercise really supports me.

Good luck finding your reflection.

"Enjoy your freedom"

Chapter 9
Stepping Out

Reconnecting emotionally, physically and visually will give you confidence to step out and back into your life. Through completing the exercises and activities in this book, you will, hopefully, have a deeper understanding of who you are, what you've gone through and the battles you have faced in your life. You have a new strength! Consequently, you may feel the need to make some bigger changes to your personal and professional life. The great thing is, you can start to see life with greater clarity. Plus, you now have a new emotional tool box which you can use to guide you back to the calmer areas of your life. This might include: friends, family, fun, adventure and work – it is all there, and you can start enjoying the life you have been waiting for.

When I stepped back, after many years of recovering, I felt strong, wise and focused. I had beaten my fear of paranoia and was loving myself. And, it was then that I found that things started to happen. I wasn't scared anymore, which was an overwhelming experience. I felt a confidence I had never felt before and a certainty that I had always wanted to feel. I no longer thought people didn't like me or were talking about me because I was comfortable with me.

My new philosophy in life is that by accepting myself, others follow suit. If they don't then it is time to side- step these people for those that do or, better still, let them side-step me. Before reconnecting with myself, I was going nowhere. Now, however, I have my life back and I am happy.

Taking small steps back into a world you have feared or felt uneasy with is a big step. But armed with confidence, self-belief and determination, you will find the power in yourself that will define you. Groundbreaking moments happen in those first few weeks of re-emerging.

Knowing what you know about yourself, who you are and how you function will lead to a more productive life that you can start enjoying. Review everything you have learnt and taught yourself. Remember what you wish to achieve in your new life with the new, stronger you.

Nothing happens overnight - we grow, gradually. By learning and discovering how best to move things forward, how to conquer situations that once drowned us, reminding ourselves our life is an extension of a past that has carved us out, we will make way for happier times.

Consolidate your personal work. You have invested heavily in your emotions, and you need to learn how to use them without them sending you back to a place you don't want to go back to. If you find a particular situation difficult to handle, then just STOP what you are doing and take a breath. Remember:

You can do this - Don't allow peer pressure to get in your way of a better life. Fight it, rise above the negativity and remove any people from your life (for the time being) who don't support you at this precious and delicate time.

Reconnecting with you- It really is vital you spend time on who you are and where you want to be, so you can really look at what has gone on in your life a little bit more objectively. Discovering and reconnecting with the person you lost sight of during your troubled times can really help you find those building blocks back to the person you want to become. By letting go of the guilt towards those causing you pain or those you might be protecting out of fear, you will discover a valuable lesson in moving forward and strengthening your mind.

Forgiveness - you don't necessarily need to forget what has happened in life, but you do need to learn to accept the painful situations in your life for what they are. These moments have defined you; you are now 'you' because of them. It is time to embrace your brilliance, the brilliant you that has been in you all this time. Keep stepping forward on the positive path towards the life you want. You have done nothing wrong. Find the strength to dig deep and release yourself from the pain. No-one controls your thoughts more than you do and it is important to grab your reins, however painful. Don't fight pain with pain.

Ring-fence your life - Identifying the people that you can take with you on your next journey is a difficult process, but one that will give you moral and trusted strength at a time when you need it. Focus on what you really want to do when you start your journey of recovery and be confident with stepping forward to make your changes. You will soon understand who is with you and who is too busy.

On the other side of fear - Do we fear change more than we fear the things in our life that cause us our anguish? Confronting our fear is our fear, and once overcome, we can fight the anxieties causing our challenges.

Your Voice – Your voice is so important. What you have to say will be heard once you understand the importance of being true to your life. Don't hide away - develop your voice to be heard. Not just listened to but really heard, and of course let your voice be seen where you need it to be.

Reflection – Enjoy what you see, physically and emotionally. Step back and enjoy you. Why not? It is your life, so connect with your body, which is giving you the life you want to lead.

Comfort Zone – When we lack confidence, we stay within our comfort zone of what we know because it is easier for us to manage. Whether it be our behaviour patterns, peer groups or routines, we find security from doing all the things that bring us comfort. However, because we fear stepping into the unknown, we never really experience our true potential. Yet, now you have read this book and reached this stage in your journey, where you might be feeling more confident, it is a great time to open yourself up to new experiences. Dare to dream. What might have once seemed impossible, might now actually feel possible.

Building Foundations Around You

As you step into the new you, full of happiness and confidence, have you thought about the foundations you have set up around you to be here today? What was it that gave you the tools to step out of your comfort zone? For example, my tool box is full of tricks to help me each day as necessary. I use my time out tool to give me constructive thoughts on difficult situations. I also give myself focused time, indulging in the things I enjoy, and I hold negativity at arm's length during my day and don't allow anyone to drain me. My boundaries are built by life and how I have learnt to become the woman I am today. I am not perfect - my journey has made me. I don't suggest for one minute I know it all, but what I do know has given me more than my survival. It has given me life.

"Living your way, matters"

Chapter 10
The New You - Enjoy!

The *new you* is here and is now part of your new life, forever. How are you going to enjoy the *new you* and how are you going to celebrate?

Time to enjoy the person you have hidden from all this time, the person you have always been but were scared to reveal; a person who has learnt the art of discernment, good judgement and appropriate responses, avoiding unnecessary dramas in the process. Refresh yourself from time-to-time on where you are going, who is important to your life and how you can manage challenging and difficult situations. Look again at your life bubble, voice bubble, your goals and hobbies, and remind yourself where you are. Your life bubble will change as time moves on; as it changes you can continue to refresh your goals and focus.

There are times when I just stop myself in my tracks. Some situations just need time to digest, think and absorb. I am a very impulsive person so for me to STOP is good. I feel that if I can just hold off and be patient for an hour or so to discern whether an action is appropriate for me to take or not, I will gain more clarity and make a grounded choice.

Also, now is the time for you to dare to dream about all the new possibilities in your life. Write your bucket list. What is it that you have always wanted to do but have never considered possible? The beauty about stepping outside what you know and outside your comfort zone is that what was once impossible becomes possible. Explore the possibilities in your life, don't hold back from experiencing every aspect of your life fully, in Technicolour!

Reading this book gives you tools to help yourself, and that for me is huge. I hope my story will help you and many others to enjoy life.

Giving Back

Now that you have rediscovered yourself and are no longer afraid or holding back, you can be a beacon of inspiration for many others. Consider what can you do to help others? Make a list of things you have taken from the book, things that you feel could be of service to other people in your life. Give back and support those who need you because there is no doubt you can. I speak to strangers, help the homeless and always wear a smile. The sky is the limit and you have an opportunity to make someone else's life richer in happiness. Where will you start?

Sharing

Sharing our knowledge is something I am very passionate about. Giving others' possibilities through reading my book is something I am very proud of. Let's work together to make others' lives happier and much more focused by what we know and what we have learnt. What did you learn from this book and how can that help someone else? You have a power now to make someone's life better. You have no restrictions on giving back, none of us have!

Be Kind to Yourself

My motto in life is to do everything with kindness. Think about how your actions affect those in your life. It doesn't take much to be kind and in fact being kind will bring a new strength to your life. I now give myself time to enjoy the things I love, such as water skiing, spas, walking, fitness and eating healthily. I also want to get some of my bucket list booked (white water rafting is high on my list) and have some fun. I have healthy boundaries and protect myself with kindness and understand when someone might be taking too much from me. My boundaries are much tighter now than they were. I can walk away from anyone or anything that creates negativity in my life. If you are in a crisis about anything, remember to use your oxygen mask first before you help others. You need to be strong before you give anymore.

Things to think about:

- *Have you had a holiday recently? Is it time to book the holiday you have always wanted?*
- *Have you been to the cinema recently?*
- *Have you an urge to be at one with Nature?*
- *Do you want to do more swimming, enjoy more walks or sporting activities?*

Whatever you now choose to do, you have to remember it is for you and your life. Don't live for others, live for you and you alone. Let life take a happier and more focused existence, with you in charge.

"Everything we want is on the other side of fear!"

Further Information about Emma-Jane Taylor

Education, Hobbies, Work, Career

As a child growing up I was super passionate about dancing, music, horse riding and animals. I was lucky enough to be involved with all my passions and performed professionally as a child dancer on many occasions. My Mum was brilliant! She took me everywhere, never gave up on me and always supported my passions and hobbies. I was lucky enough to have ponies, one on loan, *Honey* the Palomino, and my very own first pony, *Bandit*. I loved being with him. He had also been mistreated and was pretty crazy! He had no trust towards men, so we worked well together. We really understood each other's pain.

I went to a Junior School in Marlow, Buckinghamshire in the United Kingdom and a Comprehensive Girls' School in Maidenhead, Berkshire. Ironically, this school was chosen as it was closer to my Father, who lived in Maidenhead.

I failed miserably at school really. I think PE was my highest GCSE. On my last day of High School, the Headmistress invited me into her office and sat me down. She said that she would not have had me back for sixth form even if I had wanted to. She was appalled by my behaviour throughout my school years. Then I was asked to leave. Not a great end to my schooling. Looking back, I really feel sad that the school never reached out to me. I think it was clear that I was a troubled student. You can't be that naughty and happy, can you?

So, off I went into the big wide world. I felt confused, rejected, scared and thoughtful about what I should do next. I believed I should work for a big company, have a company car, earn lots of money and buy a house. My siblings all had great jobs and I believed I should follow suit. But I didn't.

My first job after leaving school sent me straight into Hairdressing, in Marlow. Sadly, after I started, I discovered I had dermatitis, which was really terrible, and had to give up my training. My first hurdle. I then decided to concentrate on earning some money and went temping, worked behind a bar, waitressed, looked after children and was generally an odd job girl. I worked hard at everything I did, but never settled anywhere.

After a year temping and because I hadn't achieved my hairdressing qualification, my sheer determination took me back to college to gain my NVQ Level II in hairdressing which I personally paid for. The dermatitis was not troubling me now I wasn't washing hair every day. I qualified and opened my mobile hairdressing business, *EJ's Mobile Hairdressing* and I was very motivated. I loved meeting people and working for myself. To supplement my income, I also worked as a Nanny, Cabaret Dancer, PA, Receptionist, Telemarketer, Waitress, Secretary, Admin Assistant and when I turned 19, I went to Menorca with the family I used to Nanny for in the UK. I liked it so much, I went for longer and stayed there for a while. I guess I was running away. I was still very troubled. In Menorca I did my hairdressing and worked as a Waitress and did some bar work. I was also a Sales Rep for a water sports company. I partied hard, had a great time, made some lifelong friends and amazingly earnt a fair bit of cash! But like all good things, I had to come back to reality.

So, at 21 I came back to the UK and got myself a, 'proper job' as a Sales Rep for a well-known photocopier company. I earnt great money, had a company car and was living the dream, but I was not happy. I really missed my dancing. I felt empty, soulless and unfulfilled. I couldn't settle. I wasn't being creative or using my passions. It was then, I knew I had to change my life.

At 23 I took a leap of faith and went back to temping, I also was asked to choreograph the Musical, *Me & My Girl* in Henley-on-Thames. I jumped at the chance. I had never choreographed a whole show before, but I knew I could. I spent many years as a child creating dances, dreaming of having my own business. The show was a success and I made some contacts. Furthermore, on the back of it, I started a tap dance class in Marlow where I lived. I also worked behind a bar, continued to temp and suddenly my life seemed full of hope, energy and desire. My passion had been fuelled. I was starting to feel happier.

At this time, I also decided to study in the fitness industry and I also decided to stop drinking alcohol. I had become more and more focused on drinking at weekends. I was spending way too much money on partying every weekend, and I started to feel massively unhappy with my alcohol consumption, the hangovers, the black outs and the loss of memory. I guess during this time I realised I was starting to understand more and more about my past and my spare weekend time was, sadly, a blur. I did have fun, but only when I was drunk. It was all so superficial. One weekend, I woke up and had literally no idea how I had got back from London. It was all fairly daunting, even with the hazy hangover, I knew things had to change.

In 1996, aged 24, I started my own business, *E-J's Dance & Fitness,* teaching tap and dance to adults. I continued as a cabaret dancer and I temped in the corporate world to continue earning regular money. I moved into teaching children's dance classes and in 2000 I opened *StageWorks Performing Arts School* for children. I wanted to give children security and stability within an environment that I had enjoyed as a child growing up. I also ended up teaching in schools and ran children's dance parties.

When I was 26 I began working more in the fitness world. I worked in an exclusive personal training gym in Beaconsfield and had the toughest of bosses who I thank every day. She gave me a steely focus and my training continued. I worked in gyms and halls and in 2013 I bought all of my fitness activities under one umbrella and I am now the Director of *NutritiousWorks*, a mobile fitness and wellbeing company.

In 2017 I collaborated with an old colleague to bring *Ocean Works Retreats* to life, an overseas retreats company focusing on wellbeing of the mind, body and soul. I had always dreamt of working overseas, as I really did miss the travel. Sadly, our relationship didn't work, but the business continues and is taking a new form over the next two years.

My work is very varied. I am also a professional Mentor, Body Transformation Coach, Personal Trainer and in 2015 I was offered the opportunity to present the *Wellbeing Show* for Oxford's, *That's TV*. I write the wellbeing column for the local newspaper and now I am an Author of my first Book, *Don't Hold Back*. I have just launched my new YouTube Channel, *The Emma Jane Taylor Show* and have also launched *SHEnetWORKS* in 2018. *SHEnetWORKS* runs empowering events, once a month, in the UK (currently Henley-on-Thames and London) and will be having a Global presence over the next few years. I am also proud to be a Co-Chair for *GYB UK London*, a global business board for Professional Women that has just launched in the UK. In 2019 I will be launching SHEnetWORKS, in London.

Everything I have learnt in life has brought me to this point in my career. I truly love my work and love where I am with everything that I am doing both professionally and personally.

The best education I've received is from, 'The University of Life'. Through my years of 'Life Education' I have had days that have undoubtedly saved me as a person and given me the skills to enjoy a life and a future that no College or University could ever have taught me.

We must also understand that what we are doing, who we think we are and what we want out of life isn't always really what we need. What we really need is to dig deep and make some much-needed changes to our world and those in it. We need to start recognising the person we know we really want to be and no longer live in a bubble of negativity and sadness.

Don't Hold Back

Testimonials from Clients

I met Emma-Jane a few months ago now. I had known of her for a while from social media but never met her until she came to my studio. I was going through a difficult time and it just felt like she had turned up at my door to help me.

We organised an initial chat to see if her mentoring would help me. My first session was emotional but expected and I felt so much lighter afterwards. I felt I was in the right place to move forward. I had about 8 sessions after that, each time talking about a certain thing. It felt like we were peeling an onion when talking about what was getting me down. Working on each thing, one at a time really helped me to deal with how I was feeling. I had got to the point where I couldn't suppress anything anymore and Emma-Jane helped me to go back and sort through it all. I feel so much better now and able to think clearly. I would totally recommend Emma-Jane's mentoring sessions for personal and business.
Ali Oswald, UK

I feel like I am flying after spending time with Emma-Jane. My career has changed direction and my relationship is more sparkly. I feel alive, bright-eyed and bushy tailed, and have such good tools to help me continue in my life.
Amanda, Oxfordshire, UK

I came to see Emma-Jane when I hit a point in life where I felt confused, full of self-doubt, trapped and just generally overwhelmed. In the sessions with Emma-Jane I would feel a release and sense of the weight being lifted. I found she listened to my needs and set realistic goals. The sessions gave me strength and courage to leave an abusive relationship that I hadn't even realised I was in. Her sessions sparked questions within myself that gave me the answers I needed. I now look back at my sessions and see how they were the perfect balance of gentle encouragement and strong focus. I needed to take a step forward to a new more positive way of living. Thank you so much Emma-Jane!

Lisa, UK

Just an evening with Emma-Jane was the start of my journey back. I have made small but significant changes and confronted all that was pulling me down. Keep doing what you are doing Emma-Jane, you are truly blessed.

Natasha, Berkshire, UK

After just one session with Emma-Jane I felt energised. She has this amazing ability to make you think differently yet positively and without guilt. She took away the heavy feeling I had been desperately holding on to and guided me through the woods to a clearing which was completely different to what I had ever expected in my life. I now feel like I can cope, my tools are powerful, and my life is enjoyable once again. I feel child-like yet emotionally strong enough to cope with anything.

Joanna, Oxfordshire, UK

It was a pleasure being interviewed by Emma-Jane on her *Wellbeing Show* for *That's Oxford TV*. Emma-Jane is friendly, yet incredibly professional and driven. Her genuine interest and passion for wellbeing shines through her engagement and thoughtful questioning. Emma-Jane exudes a certain presence, where people want to listen to her, as well as engage with her, so she is a perfect host. I can also clearly see how her background, skills and personality afford her the gravitas to take on speaking engagements across many platforms, including the corporate world. I highly recommend Emma-Jane.

Hayley Felton, UK

I've worked with Emma-Jane on several productions for TV and Video, and she's always been the ultimate professional. She clearly understands the importance of thorough preparation and hard work before filming and as a result, has an engaging, confident and relaxed on-screen persona. Her experience as a presenter allows her to adapt effortlessly to any situation as well as bringing a fresh, creative eye when needed. I'd highly recommend Emma-Jane.

Brian Naylor, UK

Contact Details

Emma-Jane Taylor
Website: www.emmajanetaylor.life
Email: theinspirationalmentor@gmail.com
Twitter: @ejthementor
Instagram: The Inspirational Mentor
Facebook: The Inspirational Mentor
LinkedIn: Emma-Jane Taylor 100 Inspirational Mentor

Businesses
StageWorks Performing Arts School
Website: www.stageworks.org.uk
Office Phone No: 01491 877205
Email: enquiries@stageworks.org.uk
Facebook: StageWorks Performing Arts School

NutritiousWorks Ltd
Website: www.nutritiousworks.com
Office Phone No: 01491 877205
Email: nutritiousworks@gmail.com
Facebook: Nutritious Works Ltd

OceanWorks Retreats
Website: www.oceanworksretreats.com
Office Phone No: 01491 877205
Email: oceanworksretreats@gmail.com
Facebook: OceanWorks Retreats

SHEnetWORKS Networking UK
Office Phone No: 01491 877205
Email: shenetworksuk@gmail.com
Facebook: Shenetworks

Emma-Jane Taylor's PA
Office Phone No: 01491 877205
Email: emmajanepa@gmail.com

Helpful Organisations

www.bacp.co.uk

www.counselling-directory.org.uk

www.nhs.uk/conditions/counselling

www.nspcc.org.uk

www.childline.org.uk

www.mind.org.uk

www.samaritans.org

Don't Hold Back

CPSIA information can be obtained
at www.ICGtesting.com
Printed in the USA
BVHW04s2201151018
530237BV00015B/168/P

9 781999 584948